# The Last Chapter

By

## Lorence A. Falkenberg

*The Last Chapter*
by Lorence A. Falkenberg

Printed in the United States of America

ISBN 978-1-60647-219-4

www.xulonpress.com

# Acknowledgments

I would like to acknowledge those who have assisted in the preparation of this book. My daughter Lee Spiess, who has typed, formatted, and edited the entire book, despite serious health issues. My wife Joyce, and my daughter Dala, who have provided material and key information, and consistently encouraged me to endure.

# Table of Contents

# Foreword

The world is steadily progressing into a society wherein God-given morals are readily ignored and shunned. Criminal activity is abounding at an unprecedented rate, there are wars and rumors of wars amongst nations, and the world is reeling in anxiety and uncertainties, to the point where man has lost the ability to control.

As time progresses towards the end of time, people are becoming more restless and aware of the end-time conditions and are seeking answers to relative questions:

- ❑ How close are we to the end of the world?
- ❑ What lies ahead for people on this earth?
- ❑ What power will bring peace and happiness?
- ❑ How can I be assured of eternal life?

Anyone who is sincerely seeking will find answers in God's Word.

A large portion of God's word, the Bible, is devoted to future end-time events, which He revealed to many prophets through the Holy Spirit. The key prophets on end-time events are Ezekiel, Daniel, and the disciple John, who wrote the book of Revelation. There are many scriptures wherein God warns us to be on guard for false prophets.

**Matthew 7:15-16**

*Beware of false prophets, who come to you in sheep's clothing, but inwardly they are ravenous wolves. You will know them by their fruits.*

Current events, particularly in the mid-east area, such as wars and rumors of wars, acts of terrorism, a mounting incensed hatred against Israel, and the development of covenants between nations in this area, are signals that the world is entering the season of the end that Christ described to His disciples.

**Matthew 24:3-8**

*Now as He sat on the Mount of Olives, the disciples came to Him privately, saying, "Tell us, when will these things be? And what will be the sign of Your coming, and of the end of the age?" And Jesus answered and said to them: "Take heed that no one deceives you. For many will come in My name, saying, 'I am the Christ,' and will deceive many. And you will hear of wars and rumors of wars. See that you are not troubled; for all these things must come to pass, but the end is not yet. For nation will rise against nation, and kingdom against kingdom. And there will be famines, pestilences, and earthquakes in various places. All these are the beginning of sorrows.*

There is no escaping the fact there is a future and an ending for the living and the dead. A study of future end-time events, based on God's own words, provides critical information as to how nations and mankind will be affected during this period in the future. Common sense tells us that man does not possess the knowledge and wisdom to predict future events. We must, therefore, consult a source that reliably reveals relative information.

The most meaningful source of information about the future lies in the hands of the Creator, the One who is omniscient. The fact that God is omniscient has been proven by the exactness and truth of the fulfilled prophecies that He gave to the prophets. God does not hide the fact that He is the only one who can foretell the future:

## II Peter 1:19-21

*And so we have the prophetic word confirmed, which you do well to heed as a light that shines in a dark place, until the day dawns and the morning star rises in your hearts; knowing this first, that no prophecy of Scripture is of any private interpretation, for prophecy never came by the will of man, but holy men of God spoke as they were moved by the Holy Spirit.*

If you want to know what lies in the future it is an absolute that you rely on an omniscient source for your information, the Word of God. Those who study the Word must cope with the immense volume of information that God has given covering the life of man from his beginning to the end of time. This volume of information is analogous to a picture puzzle, where there are many pieces that must fit together to complete the picture. So it is with the Word, you must take all of the scriptures, cross-reference them and fit them together to complete the picture, in other words:

## II Timothy 2:15

*Be diligent to present yourself approved to God, a worker who does not need to be ashamed, rightly dividing the word of truth.*

# Introduction

God revealed information about the earth's future to His servants, the prophets, through visions they had in their dreams. Angels appeared in the visions to interpret the visions and the prophets were inspired by the Holy Spirit to write what they saw and were told. When Christ began His personal ministry on earth, He taught His disciples about future events. After Christ was taken into heaven, some of the apostles spoke and wrote on these events as well. Christ's teachings and the aforementioned writings of the prophets are found in the Bible.

God's figurative and meaningful words describe the future ending of the world with sufficient details to document a reliable and conclusive picture. No codes are required to derive His intent or meaning. In His wisdom, He knew that some passages of scripture are more difficult for man to understand and referred to them as a mystery.

God has made it clear that His Word is spiritual and that natural man who is not spiritual, would not relate to it; the Word is foolishness to him. The majority of mankind have not been born of the Spirit, do not believe, but ridicule the Word and treat the Word with disrespect. This disrespect for the Word develops a mind that is closed to observing and understanding truth and reality, as it exists now and will be in the future. People who do not accept God's Word as truth, must rely on their own wisdom which is based on a carnal mind and they must go through life blindly accepting what the moment brings. There is no hope with this kind of lifestyle, and it will end when you die. If you believe in the Word, you can live life knowing what lies ahead with a hope of eternal life and a mind at peace while living on this earth.

The Bible (God's own words), has been under scrutiny of many minds and scientific research throughout time, many books are available to represent analyzed conclusions. The Bible is incomparable to any other book, with overwhelming evidence of reality and truth that could only originate from a divine author.

The Bible is a book that accurately and truthfully informs us what lies ahead for the world in which we live, as well as the eternal home that we will inherit as believers and non-believers, respectfully. We often hear the argument the Bible is not to be taken literally, and the stories and miracles that are told therein are merely allegories to guide us in life. If we place our faith in Jesus Christ and his sacrifice on our behalf, as given in the New Testament, then we must also believe in the validity of the entire scripture or our hope will be in vain.

In this book, the complex subject of the end-times has been organized into separate chapters distinguishing key issues of the subject. Scriptures, taken primarily from the books of Daniel and Revelation, support the expressed views and interpretations in this book. These scriptures have been cross-referenced with passages from other books in the bible, resulting in some repetition of scripture quotations.

The reader may find interpretations on the following topics to be new and different. They are not given in any specific order and include the:

- Battle of Gog and Magog
- Millennium
- False prophet
- Ten horns
- Harlot and the seven heads
- King of the North and South
- Four horsemen
- 75-day period
- Kingdom of clay and iron
- Five fallen kingdoms

- Judgment
- Resurrections
- Judgment Seat of Christ
- Transfer of Israel from the millennium to the new earth, and many more.

# 1: God versus Satan

The heavens and earth are God's creation of the visible and the invisible. They consist of thrones, dominions, principalities and powers.

**Colossians 1: 16-18**

*For by Him all things were created that are in heaven and that are on earth, visible and invisible, whether thrones or dominions or principalities or powers. All things were created through Him and for Him. And He is before all things, and in Him all things consist. And He is the head of the body, the church, who is the beginning, the firstborn from the dead, that in all things He may have the pre-eminence.*

Throughout the scriptures there are references to light and darkness, referring to God and Satan respectively. Light is the princi-

---

**POINT OF INTEREST**
**Lucifer – Fallen Angel**

Prior to the fall from heaven, Lucifer, the first cherub God created, was called the son of morning and he was appointed the chief angel to be in control.

*See Also:*
*Isaiah 14:12*
*Ezekiel 28:14*

After Lucifer was cast out of heaven he was called Satan and now lives in a lower realm of heaven, where he will remain until he is cast to the earth at the time of Jacob's trouble. He is now referred to as the prince of the power of the air, the spirit of disobedience.

*See Also:*
*Ephesians 2:1- 3*

His power is also described as a spiritual power of darkness.

*See Also:*
*Ephesians 6:10- 12*

---

pality of reality and truth, controlled by the spiritual powers of God. Darkness is the principalities of lies and deception, controlled by spiritual powers of Satan. These invisible spiritual powers are in conflict and are constantly affecting all of creation, but more significantly, they establish the eternal destiny of every soul.

It is assuring to know God is in control and He has bestowed all power, the greatest power known, upon Christ.

### Ephesians 1:20-21
*Which He worked in Christ when He raised Him from the dead and seated Him at His right hand in the heavenly places, far above all principality and power and might and dominion, and every name that is named, not only in this age but also in that which is to come.*

## The Mystery of God

God is omniscient He knew that man would be deceived by Satan and He had a plan that He called the *Mystery of God.*

The *Mystery of God* is His plan set before the foundation of the world, that gives everyone the opportunity to become a child of His, through the blood of His son, Christ Jesus; all who would place their faith in Him.

### Ephesians 1:4-6
*Just as He chose us in Him before the foundation of the world, that we should be holy and without blame before Him in love, having predestined us to adoption as sons by Jesus Christ to Himself, according to the good pleasure of His will, to the praise of the glory of His grace, by which He made us accepted in the Beloved.*

## Period of Grace

God does not force mankind to enter His kingdom; He allows man to choose for himself which pathway he wants to follow. As a result of this freedom, two separate families are developing, one consisting of believers in Christ and the other of non-believers in Christ. Believers are warned about the powers of darkness:

### Ephesians 6:10-12
*Finally, my brethren, be strong in the Lord and in the power of His might. Put on the whole armor of God, that you may be able to stand against the wiles of the devil. For we do not wrestle against flesh and blood, but against principalities, against powers, against the rulers of the darkness of this age, against spiritual hosts of wickedness in the heavenly places.*

During the period of grace (church age) Satan's powers and activities are curtailed to a degree by the Holy Spirit who is called *the Restrainer*. As we approach the time of the antichrist's kingdom, conditions will become more anti-Christ.

### II Timothy 3:1-5
*But know this, that in the last days perilous times will come: For men will be lovers of themselves, lovers of money, boasters, proud, blasphemers, disobedient to parents, unthankful, unholy, unloving, unforgiving, slanderers, without self-control, brutal, despisers of good, traitors, headstrong, haughty, lovers of pleasure rather than lovers of God, having a form of godliness but denying its power. And from such people turn away!*

Once the kingdom of the antichrist begins, the time period for men to find God will be approximately seven years and the conditions for those who want to become believers will be very difficult, in most cases involving a martyr's death.

### Matthew 24:9-13
*Then they will deliver you up to tribulation and kill you, and you will be hated by all nations for My name's sake. And then many will be offended, will betray one another, and will hate one another. Then many false prophets will rise up and*

*deceive many. And because lawlessness will abound, the love of many will grow cold. But he who endures to the end shall be saved.*

Our present day is the church age, known as God's period of grace. During this time, man can commit his life to Christ, exercising his faith, and by what is known as the Mystery of God, be born again; not born of flesh, but born of spirit (born again). This course of action, if undertaken, is the gift that God grants to every person through His grace. Grace is defined as giving a gift to someone without merit, or when they don't deserve it. Anyone who accepts His gift will appear faultless before God and will live for eternity with Him. The period of grace will close at mid-tribulation.

During the period of grace, the *gospel of grace* is proclaimed. There are two phases to the period of grace as follows:

1. The first phase is from the time of Christ's resurrection to the time of His appearing, at which time believers will be taken into His presence in heaven. This is commonly called the rapture of the church, and can happen at any moment.

**I Thessalonians 4:16-17**
*For the Lord Himself will descend from heaven with a shout, with the voice of an archangel, and with the trumpet of God. And the dead in Christ will rise first. Then we who are alive and remain shall be caught up together with them in the clouds to meet the Lord in the air. And thus we shall always be with the Lord.*

**I Corinthians 15:51-52**
*Behold, I tell you a mystery: We shall not all sleep, but we shall all be changed— in a moment, in the twinkling of an eye, at the last trumpet. For the trumpet will sound, and the dead will be raised incorruptible, and we shall be changed.*

2. The second phase is during the first 3 ½ years of the period of tribulation. The gospel of grace in this phase will be known

by those left behind at the rapture, from their knowledge of it during their life and friendships, together with the Word which will be in homes and libraries and the observations of the events of the rapture. Many will endure the hardships and become believers and they will be accepted by Christ at mid-tribulation. These will be martyrs.

There are distinct differences between the resurrection of the church and the resurrection of the above mentioned martyrs. The resurrection of the church (dead in Christ) happens in a moment, in the twinkling of an eye, as told in I Corinthians 15:51-52. Also noted in I Thessalonians 4:16-17.

The martyrs from the first half of the tribulation are accepted by God. They are given white robes and are under His altar and are told to rest a while longer.

### Revelation 6:9-11

*When He opened the fifth seal, I saw under the altar the souls of those who had been slain for the word of God and for the testimony which they held. And they cried with a loud voice, saying, "How long, O Lord, holy and true, until You judge and avenge our blood on those who dwell on the earth?" Then a white robe was given to each of them; and it was said to them that they should rest a little while longer, until both the number of their fellow servants and their brethren, who would be killed as they were, was completed.*

### Revelation 7:13-17

*Then one of the elders answered, saying to me, "Who are these arrayed in white robes, and where did they come from?"*

*And I said to him, "Sir, you know." So he said to me, "These are the ones who come out of the great tribulation, and washed their robes and made them white in the blood of the Lamb. Therefore they are before the throne of God, and serve Him day and night in His temple. And He who sits on the throne will dwell among them. They shall neither hunger anymore nor thirst anymore; the sun shall not strike them, nor any heat; for the Lamb who is in the midst of the throne will shepherd them and lead them to living fountains of waters. And God will wipe away every tear from their eyes.*

God's day of wrath upon the kingdom of the antichrist will begin at mid-tribulation when the seventh seal of the scroll is opened in heaven, by Christ. In the last half of the tribulation period (3 ½ years), the world will be witnessed to by the *gospel of the kingdom*, including the testimony of the two God-appointed witnesses.

### Matthew 24:14
*And this gospel of the kingdom will be preached in all the world as a witness to all the nations, and then the end will come.*

The last gospel that the world will hear is the everlasting gospel which will be preached by an angel just prior to the millennium.

### Revelation 14:6
*Then I saw another angel flying in the midst of heaven, having the everlasting gospel to preach to those who dwell on the earth—to every nation, tribe, tongue, and people—*

At the sounding of the seventh trumpet the Mystery of God will be finished. This trumpet is sounded near the start of the battle at Armageddon. After the battle at Armageddon and the judgment seat of Christ, Israel and the Gentile sheep nations will go into the millennium.

# 2: God's Figurative and Meaningful Words

The following expressions are commonly referred to in the Bible. A definition for each is given along with scriptural references, but note there is no particular order implied, nor is the list complete.

| Figurative Word | Meaning | Scripture Reference |
| --- | --- | --- |
| Stars or Prince | Angels | Daniel 10:21; Revelation 1:20 |
| Red Dragon or Red Dragon with 7 heads & 10 horns | Satan | Revelation 12:3 |
| Time of the End | Period consisting of the last days (latter days) | Daniel 8:17 |
| Gospel of Grace | The gospel message throughout the church age during the period of grace; this began with Christ's resurrection | Acts 20:24 |

| Figurative Word | Meaning | Scripture Reference |
|---|---|---|
| Gospel of the Kingdom | The gospel message preached during the second half of the tribulation period prior to the establishment of the millennium kingdom | Matthew 24:14 |
| Everlasting Gospel | The gospel preached by an angel immediately prior to the Battle at Armageddon | Revelation 14:6 |
| Was, Is Not, Yet Is | Refers to the false prophet, whose original kingdom was B.C. but during John's time he is not there, however, he is coming back in the tribulation period | Revelation 17:8-11 Daniel 9:27 |
| Woman | Nation of Israel | Revelation 12:13 |
| Great Whore / Mother of Harlots | Nations assembled under a covenant that the Antichrist will make with many. | Revelation 17:15 |
| On Wings of an Eagle | God's helping hand | Revelation 14:13; Exodus 19:4 |
| At the Appointed Time | God's appointment in time of major events; He is in control | Daniel 11:35 |
| Resurrection | The largest of many is when Christ takes the church (all believers) to be with Him | I Corinthians 15:52 |
| Bright and Morning Star | Christ will provide new Spiritual Life to believers | Revelation 2:28 |

| Figurative Word | Meaning | Scripture Reference |
|---|---|---|
| Horn | King | Daniel 8:20 |
| Saints | Israel | Psalm 50:5 |
| Michael | Chief Angel for the nation of Israel | Daniel 12:1 |
| Gabriel | Angel sent to interpret visions | Daniel 8:16 |
| Beast | Used to describe a kingdom or an individual who heads up the kingdom, the king or ruler of the kingdom | Revelation 13:1 Daniel 7:3 |
| Nation | A community of people composed of one or more nationalities with a government controlling a defined (more or less) territory | Genesis 10:1-5 Genesis 32:28 |
| Kingdom | A politically organized community or territorial unit having a monarchy government headed by a king, queen, or ruler. There may be several nations as part of the unit. In the Word, kingdoms are called beasts and their representative rulers or kings are called beasts because they control the kingdom (beast). | Daniel 2:37 |

| Figurative Word | Meaning | Scripture Reference |
|---|---|---|
| Head | A nation or past kingdom, which may unite with others to become a kingdom. These nations will act in unison with the main governing unit. | Revelation 13:1-3 |
| Kingdom of God | The everlasting kingdom, which God will set up through Christ His Son. | Revelation 11:15 |
| Sheep and Goat Nations | Sheep nations treated Israel and other nations with respect and kindness. Goat nations are those who showed no kindness. | Matthew 25:31-46 |
| Israel | Jewish nation founded on Jacob and his 12 sons – the 12 tribes. | Genesis 32:28 |
| Stone Cut without Hand | Christ | Daniel 2: 45 |
| Prince of Princes | Christ | Daniel 9:25 |
| Five Fallen | Babylon, Media-Persia, Greece, Syria, Rome Historical kingdoms that have fallen but will be re-united under covenant and become the 7 heads of the antichrist's kingdom (Great Harlot). | Revelation 17:10 |

| Figurative Word | Meaning | Scripture Reference |
|---|---|---|
| Ten Horns | Ten nations in the mid-east near Israel, each horn being a king. Three will be up-rooted by the false prophet. The ten come into power for a one hour period (literally) with the first beast. These will hate the harlot and they will make war with the Lamb. | Revelation 17:12-14 |
| Wheels | The eyes of the Lord being controlled by the four living creatures that surround God's throne. The creatures are appointed and controlled by God to observe His entire creation. I believe that the four faces of each creature, lion, ox, man and eagle, are representations of His creation and that the eyes in the rims of the wheels are the eyes of the Lord scanning the whole earth. | Ezekiel 1

Zechariah 4:10
Psalm 94:8-9 |
| Horses | God's Spirits are described as strong steeds that go into all the earth and control all affairs on earth in accordance with His will. | Zechariah 1:7-11
Zechariah 6:5-8
Revelation 6:1-8 |

# 3: Future End-time Events

The future end-time events are listed in the order of occurrence. Dates are not referred to as no one except God knows the day or the hour of the first event that will start the sequence.

**Matthew 24:36**
*But of that day and hour no one knows, not even the angels of heaven, but My Father only.*

The future events that we are expecting are as follows:

| | |
|---|---|
| 1. The appearance of Christ, when He will take believers (the Church) to heaven. | **I Thessalonians 4:16-17** |
| 2. The seven-year tribulation period will commence with the breaking of the first seal of the scroll and the kingdom of the antichrist will be established. | **Revelation 6:1-2 & Revelation 13:1-9** |
| 3. The many judgments of God are poured out throughout the first half of the tribulation period. | **Revelation 6** |
| 4. The Sealing of the 144,000 Jews at mid-tribulation. | **Revelation 7:1-8** |

| | |
|---|---|
| 5. The Resurrection of the millions who died in the first half of the tribulation. | **Revelation 7:9-17** |
| 6. The false prophet will appear at the mid-point of the tribulation. | **Revelation 13:11-18** |
| 7. The second half of the tribulation starts with the breaking of the seventh seal and God's day of wrath begins. | **Revelation 8:1** |
| 8. The ministry of God's two witnesses begins at mid-tribulation. | **Revelation 11:1-14** |
| 9. Satan is thrown out of heaven. | **Revelation 12:7-17** |
| 10. God's judgments and wrath commencing at mid-tribulation through to the seventh bowl of wrath. | **Revelation Chapters 8-16** |
| 11. Judgment of Babylon the Great. | **Revelation 17:1-18** |
| 12. The marriage of the Lamb. | **Revelation 19:9** |
| 13. The Battle at Armageddon. | **Revelation 19:11-21** |
| 14. Satan is bound and the millennium begins. | **Revelation 20:1-6** |
| 15. Satan is released and the battle of Gog and Magog occurs. | **Revelation 20:7-10** |
| 16. The Great White Throne of Judgment is conducted. | **Revelation 20:11-15** |
| 17. God will create new Heavens and a new earth. | **Revelation 21:1-8** |

| 18. New Jerusalem comes to the new earth. | **Revelation 21:9-27** |
|---|---|
| 19. The River of Life. | **Revelation 22:1-5** |

Anyone who is interested in end-times must know that the events fall into the time frame of the future and that they will take place by God's timing and direction. Prime, targeted events will occur mainly in the mid-east area, where the antichrist will establish his kingdom. This is the area where creation and the population of mankind had its beginning; specifically, the Garden of Eden. This is also the area in the end-times, where the nation of Israel will be gathered by God from all parts of the earth, in order that they may inherit their kingdom in the land that was promised to Abraham. Prior to the re-gathering, Israel will be the epicenter of horrendous experiences under the rule of the antichrist, particularly during the last 3 ½ years of the tribulation period. After the climaxing battle at Armageddon, Israel will be re-gathered from all parts of the earth, to establish Christ's everlasting kingdom on earth; this is known as the millennium.

# 4: God's Control and Intervention

There are three distinct major events, all of which are under God's control and commands. These future events will commence at God's command and the world will encounter assumed and specific consequences when each event occurs.

**First Major Event**

### I Thessalonians 4: 16-18
*For the Lord Himself will descend from heaven with a shout, with the voice of an archangel, and with the trumpet of God. And the dead in Christ will rise first. Then we who are alive and remain shall be caught up together with them in the clouds to meet the Lord in the air. And thus we shall always be with the Lord. Therefore comfort one another with these words.*

This act will happen quickly, when believers are transformed into spiritual beings:

### I Corinthians 15:51-52
*Behold, I tell you a mystery: We shall not all sleep, but we shall all be changed - in a moment, in the twinkling of an eye, at the last trumpet. For the trumpet will sound, and the dead will be raised incorruptible, and we shall be changed.*

Prior to the commencement of the tribulation period, God will take the church out of the earth.

## Assumed Consequences of the First Major Event

### Physical Chaos

When all believers are taken in a moment, in the twinkling of an eye, there will be accidents of every kind, injuries, dead bodies to bury, fires and floods. The destruction left by natural disasters such as hurricanes and tornados, are small in comparison. Required emergency services will also be curtailed as a result of missing people who have been taken. The conditions on earth will be in chaos and ripe for the antichrist to offer his deceptive leadership to the world.

### Mental Chaos

Everyone's mind will be in anxiety and discomfort when they realize that they were left behind. There will be grieving over lost family members and friends, and loneliness coupled with fear, as people scramble to cope with conditions of disaster and lawlessness. As time progresses, there will arise feelings of mistrust. There will be feuding over the possessions and properties of those who were raptured.

## Second Major Event

God allows Satan and the antichrists to establish a kingdom on the earth for a period of seven years, known as the period of tribulation; a time when God will exercise His judgments and wrath upon Satan and his followers. God's wrath will commence at mid-tribulation, when the Holy Spirit will stop restraining Satan.

### II Thessalonians 2:7

*For the mystery of lawlessness is already at work; only He who now restrains will do so until He is taken out of the way.*

Satan will empower two individuals with his powers of darkness. These individuals force people to honor them and live according to the standards of darkness which they will control.

Satan's kingdom will begin when the first seal of the scroll is opened, the scroll God is holding in His right hand. Satan, the Red Dragon with seven heads and ten horns, will empower the antichrist (ruler – king) to begin his reign on the earth. This kingdom begins with the seven heads and at mid-tribulation will have the ten horns (kings) added to it.

## Specific Consequences of the Second Major Event

### Kingdom of Darkness

Once the kingdom of the antichrist is set up people will be living under his rule. They will be forced to worship the antichrist and will not have churches to worship in; they will be living with the spirit of darkness. Men who want to believe in God will be killed as martyrs by the antichrist.

Living conditions on the earth will be extreme and horrible; men will be forced to live by the laws and decrees set up by the antichrist, while he will wage war.

### Revelation 6:2

*And I looked, and behold, a white horse. He who sat on it had a bow; and a crown was given to him, and he went out conquering and to conquer.*

Conditions will be troubled and there will be no peace:

### Revelation 6:4

*Another horse, fiery red, went out. And it was granted to the one who sat on it to take peace from the earth, and that people should kill one another; and there was given to him a great sword.*

There will be a shortage of food:

### Revelation 6:5-6
*When He opened the third seal, I heard the third living crea-*
*ture say, "Come and see." So I looked, and behold, a black*
*horse, and he who sat on it had a pair of scales in his hand.*
*And I heard a voice in the midst of the four living creatures*
*saying, "A quart of wheat for a denarius, and three quarts*
*of barley for a denarius; and do not harm the oil and the*
*wine."*

Conditions near the end of the first half of the tribulation will be a time of intense warfare in the mid-east area, involving starvation and killing with beasts:

### Revelation 6:8
*So I looked, and behold, a pale horse. And the name of him*
*who sat on it was Death, and Hades followed with him. And*
*power was given to them over a fourth of the earth, to kill*
*with sword, with hunger, with death, and by the beasts of the*
*earth.*

### Third Major Event

God will establish His own kingdom on the earth for Israel. This kingdom will fulfill the covenant He made with Israel and the kingdom will stand forever. This kingdom on earth will begin with one thousand years of peace on earth (the millennium) when Satan will be bound in chains and placed into the bottomless pit. Christ will hold the judgment of nations and He will decide which nations are sheep and which ones are goats. The decision will be based on the way the nations have treated and respected Israel and each other. The sheep nations (those who were kind and respectful to other nations) are allowed to enter His kingdom.

Administration of His kingdom on earth will be designated to Israel under King David, but control and power will lie in the hands of Christ who will rule with a rod of iron. At the end of the millennium, peace will be interrupted when Satan is released from the bottomless pit and he will deceive all nations to come to war against Israel. This will be the last battle on earth and it is known as the battle of Gog and Magog. Men and nations who lived through the millennium and did not keep God's standards, are again deceived by Satan and will meet God at the Great White Throne of Judgment together with all non-believers.

The church, which was taken into heaven at the resurrection of believers, has already become a part of the kingdom of God located in heaven.

# 5: Israel

As mentioned previously, God's plan, which was set before the foundation of the world, was for Jesus Christ, His own Son, to enter the world as a man and become a sacrifice as payment for man's sin. Christ's entry as a man, into the world, came through the lineage of Israel, the nation God chose for this purpose; Israel is God's chosen nation, above all others, the apple of His eye.

**Zechariah 2:8**

*For thus says the LORD of hosts: "He sent Me after glory, to the nations which plunder you; for he who touches you touches the apple of His eye.*

In scripture we are told that Israel is Satan's enemy, consequently it will be under constant attack, experiencing extraordinary hardships, particularly during the period of tribulation which will be ruled by the antichrist.

---

**POINT OF INTEREST**
Israel in History

2. Israel escaped from Egypt by crossing the Red Sea with God's help. Highly recommended viewing is the DVD The Search for the Real Mt. Sinai. Check out: www.reelproductions.net

3. Israel was persecuted by the Assyrians.

4. Israel was captured and lived under the rule or influence of the historical kingdoms of Babylon, Media-Persia, Greece, Syria, and Rome. The actual account of history during this long period is not critical to understand the future end-time events, but an understanding of the role these past kingdoms will have in the future is very relevant and significant in unfolding a meaningful interpretation of the last kingdom which will be the kingdom of the Antichrist that Israel and the world will have to contend with in the future.

---

Israel's rejection of God led to a life of slavery under the rule of historical kingdoms. Historical kingdoms that lived out their existence prior, will return and again have a role in the events of the future. The countries that existed in B.C. are still there, although some have different names today, i.e., Babylon is Iraq, Media-Persia is Iran. The book of Daniel provides information on historical kingdoms and their relevance to the understanding of future events described in the book of Revelation.

## Israel Under Syrian and Roman Rule

In approximately 160 B.C., Israel was devastated by the Syrian ruler Antiochus Epiphanes who destroyed Israel's temple and created spiritual desolation within the nation that still exists today. Antiochus Epiphanes sacrificed a pig on the altar in Israel's temple, which set up what is known in biblical terms as *the abomination of desolation*. The second phase of Israel's spiritual desolation came as a result of the Roman attack when it's temple was destroyed and Israel was dispersed throughout the world.

### Daniel 9:26
*And after the sixty-two weeks Messiah shall be cut off, but not for Himself; and the people of the prince who is to come shall destroy the city and the sanctuary. The end of it shall be with a flood, and till the end of the war desolations are determined.*

Israel remains dispersed for approximately 2000 years.

## Partial Re-Gathering of Israel

During recent years, Jewish people returned to Israel by their own choice and in 1948, Israel was officially recognized as a nation. After this partial and voluntary re-gathering, Israel has become a nation that is fully armed, being attacked and threatened by surrounding nations. Israel is not living in peace, nor will it be from today through the seven year period of tribulation, which is climaxed at the battle at Armageddon. Israel is not living in un-walled villages and in peace, but rather will be driven out of it's land into the wilderness where God will protect and provide for the people.

### Revelation 12:14
*But the woman was given two wings of a great eagle, that she might fly into the wilderness to her place, where she is nourished for a time and times and half a time, from the presence of the serpent.*

## Full Re-Gathering of Israel

The full re-gathering of Israel is not voluntary, it is a future act of God performed after the battle at Armageddon. This re-gathering is described in Ezekiel and Isaiah.

### Ezekiel 36:34
*For I will take you from among the nations, gather you out of all countries, and bring you into your own land.*

### Ezekiel 37:21-28
*"Then say to them, 'Thus says the Lord GOD: "Surely I will take the children of Israel from among the nations, wherever they have gone, and will gather them from every side and bring them into their own land; and I will make them one nation in the land, on the mountains of Israel; and one king shall be king over them all; they shall no longer be two nations, nor shall they ever be divided into two kingdoms again. They shall not defile themselves anymore with their idols, nor with their detestable things, nor with any of their transgressions; but I will deliver them from all their dwelling places in which they have sinned, and will cleanse them. Then they shall be My people, and I will be their God. "David My servant shall be king over them, and they shall all have one shepherd; they shall also walk in My judgments and observe My statutes, and do them. Then they shall dwell in the land that I have given to Jacob My servant, where your*

*fathers dwelt; and they shall dwell there, they, their children, and their children's children, forever; and My servant David shall be their prince forever. Moreover I will make a covenant of peace with them, and it shall be an everlasting covenant with them; I will establish them and multiply them, and I will set My sanctuary in their midst forevermore. My tabernacle also shall be with them; indeed I will be their God, and they shall be My people. The nations also will know that I, the LORD, sanctify Israel, when My sanctuary is in their midst forevermore."*

### Isaiah 49:22
*Thus says the Lord GOD: " Behold, I will lift My hand in an oath to the nations, and set up My standard for the peoples; they shall bring your sons in their arms, and your daughters shall be carried on their shoulders;*

God will use nations to accomplish the full re-gathering and He will set up the everlasting kingdom, which is the millennium. During the millennium, Israel will be living in peace and in un-walled villages, a time when Christ will be ruling with a rod of iron. The distinct contrast between the partial re-gathering and full re-gathering of Israel must be taken into account to clearly understand the truth in God's words. The battle at Armageddon and the battle of Gog and Magog are 1000 years apart. The battle at Armageddon occurs at the end of the tribulation period. The battle of Gog and Magog occurs at the end of the millennium.

### Revelation 20:7-9
*Now when the thousand years have expired, Satan will be released from his prison and will go out to deceive the nations which are in the four corners of the earth, Gog and Magog, to gather them together to battle, whose number is as the sand of the sea. They went up on the breadth of the earth and surrounded the camp of the saints and the beloved city. And fire came down from God out of heaven and devoured them.*

## Israel Today

The world is currently living in the short period of time between the remaining time of the *Church Age* and the beginning of the antichrist's kingdom, which will trigger seven years of tribulation. The end of the Church Age and the start of the antichrist's kingdom are events that are under God's control and timing. Both will significantly impact Israel when they occur.

Today, Israel is fully armed and fighting for its existence. It is being attacked by surrounding nations and under duress from western nations to negotiate, for the sake of peace, by relinquishing land it conquered in recent wars. Under these stressful conditions Israel maintains its desire to rebuild the temple on the site of the original temple. The ultimate outcome of negotiations for peace may result in Israel acquiring the necessary land and the right to rebuild its temple.

The rebuilding of the temple is not merely an abstract thought. Both current events and scripture lend credence to the reality for this event. Most importantly, the words of God indicate that Israel will be worshipping, through sacrifice and offering, during the first 3 ½ years of tribulation and infer that Israel will be involved in the negotiation of the covenant the antichrist establishes with many.

### Daniel 9:27

*Then he shall confirm a covenant with many for one week; but in the middle of the week he shall bring an end to sacrifice and offering. And on the wing of abominations shall be one who makes desolate, even until the consummation, which is determined, is poured out on the desolate."*

My view is that Israel will rebuild the temple and establish its worship and sacrifice prior to the start of the tribulation, because the antichrist, at his inception will proclaim to be God.

### Daniel 11:36

*"Then the king shall do according to his own will: he shall exalt and magnify himself above every god, shall speak blas-*

*phemies against the God of gods, and shall prosper till the
wrath has been accomplished; for what has been determined
shall be done. He shall regard neither the God of his fathers
nor the desire of women, nor regard any god; for he shall
exalt himself above them all. But in their place he shall honor
a god of fortresses; and a god which his fathers did not know
he shall honor with gold and silver, with precious stones
and pleasant things. Thus he shall act against the strongest
fortresses with a foreign god, which he shall acknowledge,
and advance its glory; and he shall cause them to rule over
many, and divide the land for gain.*

### Revelation 13:5-7
*And he was given a mouth speaking great things and blas-
phemies, and he was given authority to continue for forty-
two months. Then he opened his mouth in blasphemy against
God, to blaspheme His name, His tabernacle, and those who
dwell in heaven. It was granted to him to make war with the
saints and to overcome them. And authority was given him
over every tribe, tongue, and nation.*

It is highly unlikely that the antichrist will allow Israel to build
a temple any time during his reign. It is the false prophet who
will put an end to Israel's worship and sacrifice at mid-tribulation
(mid-week).

### II Thessalonians 2:4
*...who opposes and exalts himself above all that is called
God or that is worshiped, so that he sits as God in the temple
of God, showing himself that he is God.*

Near the end of the tribulation period, the false prophet will sit
in the temple and proclaim to be God.

An interesting question arises: will the temple be rebuilt prior to
the rapture of the church? There is no clear answer to which event
will occur first, however, both events will occur before the tribulation. Only God knows the timing of the events and only He knows

the exact nature of the attacks and wars that Israel must endure prior to and during the tribulation.

Israel's future does not look bright. Consider the changes that only three soon-to-occur events will have on Israel; firstly, the removal of western troops from the mid-east area; secondly, the removal the church and restraining power of the Holy Spirit from the world; thirdly, the beginning of the rule of the antichrist.

During the first 3 ½ years of the tribulation period, Israel and the world will be living under the rule of the antichrist, who from the beginning will be at war, expanding his kingdom with the newly established power base of the seven heads, the seven nations under his covenant, including the four Muslim nations of Iraq, Iran, Syria, and Turkey. Discussion of the power base is given in the discussion of the kingdom of the antichrist.

> **POINT OF INTEREST**
> **Times of Stress, Turmoil & War**
> 1. The comfort of true Christian companionship, kindness and support will be removed from the world by the resurrection of the church (rapture). Israel and the world will be in stressful condition's which worsen until mid-tribulation, when God's day of wrath begins.
> 2. The Holy Spirit is restraining Satan until mid-tribulation when the man of sin (false prophet) is revealed. Please note that the Antichrist was granted permission by God to go to war with Israel during the first half of the tribulation period.
> *See Also:*
> *Revelation 13:7*
> *II Thessalonians 2:7-12*
> *Revelation 17:8*

God's four spirits, who are the four horses of Revelation 6, will allow war, removal of peace, famines, killing and death. The world will marvel and follow the beast and worship the dragon and boast that no one can make war against this kingdom. The antichrist will continue this boasting by blaspheming God and the worship of God. He will go to war with Israel and overcome them. The whole world will be forced to worship him. In the first half of the tribulation period a great multitude will be martyred for refusing to worship the beast. Please refer to the discussion on the opening of the fifth seal in Revelation 6.

Immediately prior to the day of wrath there will be a great earthquake, the sun will go black, the moon will become red like blood, stars will fall, the sky will disappear and every mountain and island will be moved. Men will seek hiding places as they will be in great fear. At this time, the Holy Spirit will stop restraining Satan and control of the antichrist's kingdom will transfer to the false prophet and God's day of wrath will begin. When the seventh seal of His scroll is opened, God's wrath will be poured out on the world at the appointed times of the sounding of seven trumpets.

During the last half of the tribulation Israel will be subjected to God's horrific judgements as well as a life of cruelty under the rule of the false prophet. Prior to the start of the 3 ½ year period of wrath, 144,000 men from the twelve tribes of Israel will receive God's seal on their foreheads which will protect them and allow them to survive the unbearable conditions. During this period God will send His two witnesses, Elijah and John, to preach the gospel of the kingdom. Anyone who decides to receive this gospel will be required to endure unto the end and will become martyrs.

At the beginning of the 75 day period (Jacob's time of trouble), the false prophet will implement the abomination of desolation for the second time and will sit in the temple proclaiming to be God. He will be performing great signs, bringing fire down from heaven and giving breath to the image he will build in honour of the antichrist. This image will appear to be alive because it will speak; a feat that will not be impossible considering the technology of our day. The false prophet will force people to take the mark of the beast on their right hands or foreheads and anyone who does not accept the mark will not be able to buy or sell. It will be a time of marshal reign, when the cruel leadership of the false prophet will be killing people that will not worship Satan and accept the mark. This will be a time when people will be betrayed by their own families who become informers.

**Mark 13:12**
*Now brother will betray brother to death, and a father his child; and children will rise up against parents and cause them to be put to death.*

The worst woe of all time will come upon Israel when Satan and his fallen angels will be cast from heaven to earth, to persecute Israel causing the nation to flee into the wilderness. Only God's protection upon Israel will prevent complete annihilation.

**Jeremiah 30:7**
*Alas! For that day is great, so that none is like it; and it is the time of Jacob's trouble, but he shall be saved out of it.*

**See Also**:

❑ Revelation 12:6
❑ Revelation 12:14
❑ Daniel 12:7

The seven last plagues imposed upon the world are introduced as *bowl judgments* immediately prior to the battle at Armageddon. Refer to Revelation 16 to read of the atrocities and the earth-shaking events that will lead the nations into the battle at Armageddon. After the battle at Armageddon, God will re-gather Israel from all parts of the earth, and they will enter the millennium.

# 6: The Kingdom of the Antichrist

The future kingdom of the antichrist, which God refers to as *the great harlot*, has its roots in the city of Babel in the land of Shinar (Babylon).

### Genesis 11: 1-9

*Now the whole earth had one language and one speech. And it came to pass, as they journeyed from the east, that they found a plain in the land of Shinar, and they dwelt there. Then they said to one another, "Come, let us make bricks and bake them thoroughly." They had brick for stone, and they had asphalt for mortar. And they said, "Come, let us build ourselves a city, and a tower whose top is in the heavens; let us make a name for ourselves, lest we be scattered abroad over the face of the whole earth." But the LORD came down to see the city and the tower which the sons of men had built. And the LORD said, "Indeed the people are one and they all have*

> **POINT OF INTEREST**
> **Wicked Woman – The Harlot**
> The angel who spoke to Zechariah in a vision, referred to the Antichrist's kingdom as a wicked woman: *"This is Wickedness"*; so wicked that she was thrust into a basket with a lid of lead. The basket with the wicked woman will eventually be delivered to its base in the land of Shinar, when the base is ready. The land of Shinar is near Babylon (in Iraq). This is where the permanent headquarters of the Antichrist will be.
> *Daniel 11:45*: *"and he shall plant the tents of his palace between the seas and the glorious holy mountain; yet he shall come to his end, and no one will help him."*

*one language, and this is what they begin to do; now nothing that they propose to do will be withheld from them. Come, let Us go down and there confuse their language, that they may not understand one another's speech." So the LORD scattered them abroad from there over the face of all the earth, and they ceased building the city. Therefore its name is called Babel, because there the LORD confused the language of all the earth; and from there the LORD scattered them abroad over the face of all the earth.*

Babylon was the mother of the harlot and of the abomination of the earth. Her abominations have prevailed, and will continue to prevail, in the kings and kingdoms on earth, culminating into the next and last kingdom on earth, the kingdom of the antichrist. The antichrist's kingdom is referred to as follows:

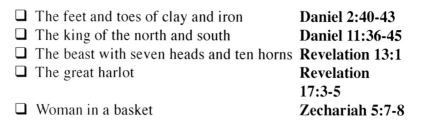

❑ The feet and toes of clay and iron    **Daniel 2:40-43**
❑ The king of the north and south    **Daniel 11:36-45**
❑ The beast with seven heads and ten horns **Revelation 13:1**
❑ The great harlot    **Revelation 17:3-5**

❑ Woman in a basket    **Zechariah 5:7-8**

God used the word *mystery* when He named the great harlot because development of this future kingdom is lengthy and complex, involving all historical kingdoms. He also refers to this line of kingdoms as *that great city* in Revelation 17:18. The development of the antichrist's kingdom is ongoing today and in Matthew 24, Christ gave his disciples an overview of the conditions that will be prevalent near the time that this kingdom will come into power.

### Matthew 24: 4-8

*And Jesus answered and said to them: "Take heed that no one deceives you. For many will come in My name, saying, 'I am the Christ,' and will deceive many. And you will hear of wars and rumors of wars. See that you are not troubled; for all these things must come to pass, but the end is not yet. For nation will rise against nation, and kingdom against kingdom. And there will be famines, pestilences, and earthquakes in various places. All these are the beginning of sorrows.*

The following conditions in the world today correspond to Christ's overview, substantiating that the kingdom of the antichrist is coming into place:

- Earthquakes in diverse places, proliferation of false cults including schools dedicated specifically to atheism, wars and rumours of wars, famines, pestilences, murders and thievery as a common lifestyle.
- The wounded head of the beast (Iraq) (Revelation 13:3)
- Nations are establishing covenants (Iran, Syria, Lebanon)
- Nations have the desire and plans to annihilate Israel (Iran)
- Israel's plans to re-build the temple (the antichrist will stop Israel's worship and sacrifice during the tribulation period)
- The world is developing a pronounced spirit of antichrist with Satan worship.

Christ's overview continued through the period of tribulation (**Matthew 24: 9 - 44**). He then gave the disciples a parable that constitutes a time frame for all of the above to happen – *The Budding of the Fig Tree.*

The reference of the *budding of the fig tree,* which includes the world conditions leading up to the establishment of the antichrist's kingdom and the seven year rule of the antichrists, indicates it will all happen in one generation; a period of 20 to 25 years. The antichrist will form his kingdom by uniting a group of nations under a covenant.

### Daniel 9:27

*Then he shall confirm a covenant with many for one week; but in the middle of the week he shall bring an end to sacrifice and offering. And on the wing of bominations shall be one who makes desolate, even until the nsummation, which is determined, is poured out on the desolate."*

The nations under covenant are the seven heads of the kingdom (the beast of Revelation 13:1) and are synonymous with the great harlot that will be the first part of the antichrist's kingdom and also with the King of the North.

### Daniel 11:36-45

*Then the king shall do according to his own will: he shall exalt and magnify himself above every god, shall speak blasphemies against the God of gods, and shall prosper till the wrath has been accomplished; for what has been determined shall be done. He shall regard neither the God of his fathers nor*

> **POINT OF INTEREST**
> Parable of the Fig Tree –
> **God's Control & Timeframe**
> *Matthew 24: 32-35*
> Christ said the development of the beast and its lifespan through the seven years of tribulation concluding with the battle at Armageddon will take place in one generation. Accepting that a generation is approximately 20 – 25 years, one can see that the time is near, particularly when you take into account many conditions for forming the antichrist's kingdom are happening now.
> The official rule of the antichrist will begin when God allows the first seal, of the scroll He is holding in His hand, to be opened. At that time the beast's rule will begin and will last for seven years, also stated to be 42 months or 2520 days (1260 days in the first half and 1260 days in the second half of the tribulation period), plus the 75-day period of *Jacob's time of trouble.*

*the desire of women, nor regard any god; for he shall exalt himself above them all. But in their place he shall honor a god of fortresses; and a god which his fathers did not know he shall honor with gold and silver, with precious stones and pleasant things. Thus he shall act against the strongest fortresses with a foreign god, which he shall acknowledge, and advance its glory; and he shall cause them to rule over many, and divide the land for gain. "At the time of the end the king of the South shall attack him; and the king of the North shall come against him like a whirlwind, with chariots, horsemen, and with many ships; and he shall enter the countries, overwhelm them, and pass through. He shall also enter the Glorious Land, and many countries shall be over-thrown; but these shall escape from his hand: Edom, Moab, and the prominent people of Ammon. He shall stretch out his hand against the countries, and the land of Egypt shall not escape. He shall have power over the treasures of gold and silver, and over all the precious things of Egypt; also the Libyans and Ethiopians shall follow at his heels. But news from the east and the north shall trouble him; therefore he shall go out with great fury to destroy and annihilate many. And he shall plant the tents of his palace between the seas and the glorious holy mountain; yet he shall come to his end, and no one will help him.*

## Components of the Antichrist's Kingdom

The kingdom of the antichrist, consists of three components as follows:

- Satan – the red dragon with seven heads and ten horns
- Seven Heads – seven nations under covenant, united, ruled by the King of the North, and also known as The Great Harlot
- Ten Horns – ten nations receiving kingdoms from the King of the North, near mid-tribulation. The ten horns will become seven when the false prophet uproots three of the ten. These horns (nations) are a second component of the antichrist's kingdom, becoming part of the antichrist's kingdom near mid-tribulation. They rule with the antichrist for one hour prior to be taken over by the false prophet. They are referred to as the King of the South, and will be forced to join the King of the North after they lose the war against him. They hate the harlot (King of the North).

### Satan
Satan is described as the red dragon having seven heads and ten horns and seven diadems on his heads. His host includes one third of the angels who chose to go with him.

### Revelation 12:3-4
*And another sign appeared in heaven: behold, a great, fiery red dragon having seven heads and ten horns, and seven diadems on his heads. His tail drew a third of the stars of heaven and threw them to the earth. And the dragon stood before the woman who was ready to give birth, to devour her Child as soon as it was born.*

Satan is the spiritual power of darkness that controls the affairs of non-believing mankind on the earth. He started exercising his powers of darkness after he fell with his pride before God in heaven. From the time of his influence in the Garden of Eden, he has continued to influence mankind throughout time and in all kingdoms of history. The seven diadems on his head are representative of kings that he controlled in the past, whose nations will ultimately join in covenant to form the future kingdom of the antichrist with seven heads. Near the end of the tribulation period Satan is cast from heaven and the last phase of the antichrist's kingdom will be formed, referred to as the *Feet and Toes of Iron and Clay.*

### Daniel 2:41
*Whereas you saw the feet and toes, partly of potter's clay and partly of iron, the kingdom shall be divided; yet the strength of the iron shall be in it, just as you saw the iron mixed with ceramic clay.*

The latter part of the kingdom will become divided when Satan is cast to earth, and the kingdom will be partly strong and partly fragile due to the clay, which is Satan and his fallen angels. This kingdom will go to the battle at Armageddon, and after the battle Satan will be bound in chains and cast into the bottomless pit. 1000 years later Satan will eventually be destroyed in the battle of Gog and Magog and will be cast into the lake of fire after that battle.

### Seven Heads
The seven heads are seven nations who will be part of a covenant that will be organized by the antichrist to form a power base for his

kingdom. The covenant will last for seven years. This power base is called king of the north in Daniel, called the kingdom with seven heads and ten horns in Revelation, and also referred to as the great harlot in Revelation.

### Daniel 9:27
*Then he shall confirm a covenant with many for one week....*

To understand the component of seven heads one must refer to and cross-reference information given in the following scriptures:

- Daniel Chapters 2, 7, 8, 9, 10, 11, 12 and Revelation Chapters 13, 17, and 18.

### See Also:

❑ *Information given in Revelation Chapter 17 in this book, regarding the seven heads.*

### The Seven Heads - The King of the North, The Great Harlot
The kingdom itself will begin with the seven heads, seven nations under covenant, who will be at war in the mid-east area and will gain control of the area. The king's activities are described in Daniel 11:36-39, where in this reference the antichrist is the king of the north.

### Daniel 11:36-39
*"Then the king shall do according to his own will: he shall exalt and magnify himself above every god, shall speak blasphemies against the God of gods, and shall prosper till the wrath has been accomplished; for what has been determined shall be done. He shall regard neither the God of his fathers nor the desire of women, nor regard any god; for he shall exalt himself above them all. But in their place he shall honor*

*a god of fortresses; and a god which his fathers did not know he shall honor with gold and silver, with precious stones and pleasant things. Thus he shall act against the strongest fortresses with a foreign god, which he shall acknowledge, and advance its glory; and he shall cause them to rule over many, and divide the land for gain.*

During his conquests he will divide the land for gain and no one will be able to make war with him. This part of the antichrist's kingdom is the part that is partly of iron, the part that has strength in it.

Please note the following about the king who will be the antichrist. He will:

- Be a dictator and exalt himself above all
- Be blasphemous against God
- Establish a strange god - himself under his own declaration
- Plant the tents of his palace between the seas in the mid-east

### Ten Horns

The ten horns will arise from the fourth kingdom which will devour the whole earth and break it to pieces. The fourth kingdom began with the Roman empire, the kingdom of iron. This major empire fell at Pergamos, but remnants of the empire are ongoing today, as the *one is* kingdom, from which the ten horns will arise.

### Revelation 17:10-14

*There are also seven kings. Five have fallen, one is, and the other has not yet come. And when he comes, he must continue a short time. The beast that was, and is not, is himself also the eighth, and is of the seven, and is going to perdition. "The ten horns which you saw are ten kings who have received no kingdom as yet, but they receive authority for one hour as kings with the beast. These are of one mind, and they will give their power and authority to the beast. These will make war with the Lamb, and the Lamb will overcome them, for*

*He is Lord of lords and King of kings; and those who are with Him are called, chosen, and faithful."*

## Daniel 7:24
*The ten horns are ten kings who shall arise from this kingdom. And another shall rise after them; he shall be different from the first ones, and shall subdue three kings.*

These kings will reign for one hour with the antichrist, and when the false prophet comes, he will subdue three of the ten.

## Revelation 17:8
*The beast that you saw was, and is not, and will ascend out of the bottomless pit and go to perdition. And those who dwell on the earth will marvel, whose names are not written in the Book of Life from the foundation of the world, when they see the beast that was, and is not, and yet is.*

## Revelation 17:12
*"The ten horns which you saw are ten kings who have received no kingdom as yet, but they receive authority for one hour as kings with the beast.*

The false prophet takes leadership from the antichrist at midtribulation; he is, therefore, leader of the seven heads which represent the King of the North. Very likely the false prophet uproots three of the ten horns after he (King of the North) is victorious in the war between the King of the North and the King of the South, described in Daniel Chapter 11. This is a civil war between the components of the antichrist's kingdom.

The ten Muslim nations who will be the King of the South are in animosity with the King of the North because the King of the North does not worship Allah, even though Iraq, Iran, Syria, and Turkey are part of the King of the North. The King of the North has set himself up as the god his fathers never knew, a strange god. The animosity between the Kings of the South and North is referred to in Revelation 17.

### Revelation 17:16
*And the ten horns which you saw on the beast, these will hate the harlot, make her desolate and naked, eat her flesh and burn her with fire.*

This animosity will result in the war described in Daniel 11.

### Daniel 11:40-45
*"At the time of the end the king of the South shall attack him; and the king of the North shall come against him like a whirlwind, with chariots, horsemen, and with many ships; and he shall enter the countries, overwhelm them, and pass through. He shall also enter the Glorious Land, and many countries shall be overthrown; but these shall escape from his hand: Edom, Moab, and the prominent people of Ammon. He shall stretch out his hand against the countries, and the land of Egypt shall not escape. He shall have power over the treasures of gold and silver, and over all the precious things of Egypt; also the Libyans and Ethiopians shall follow at his heels. But news from the east and the north shall trouble him; therefore he shall go out with great fury to destroy and annihilate many. And he shall plant the tents of his palace between the seas and the glorious holy mountain; yet he shall come to his end, and no one will help him.*

After the king of the North wins the war, the ten horns will be compelled to give their authority to the beast.

### Revelation 17:17
*For God has put it into their hearts to fulfill His purpose, to be of one mind, and to give their kingdom to the beast, until the words of God are fulfilled.*

This is the time when the false prophet uproots three of the other horns, the time that he builds the image in honour of the first beast, enforces the mark of the beast, and sets up the abomination of desolation for the second time. The ten horns of Daniel 7:24, are the ten toes of Daniel 2:44 and the ten horns of Revelation 17:12

In Daniel Chapter 2, the ten toes are described as a kingdom that is divided (King of the North and King of the South), a kingdom that is part iron and part clay, iron remnants of the Roman empire will be mixed with clay, clay being Satan and his fallen angels. Clay and iron don't mix but both elements will be smitten by Christ at Armageddon.

### Daniel 2:43

*As you saw iron mixed with ceramic clay, they will mingle with the seed of men; but they will not adhere to one another, just as iron does not mix with clay.*

The timing of the war in heaven between Michael and Satan, is the time when the clay for the ten toes comes into existence. The ten toes of Daniel 2 are the feet and toes destroyed at the battle at Armageddon and the war in heaven happens just prior to the 75 day period of Jacob's time of trouble immediately prior to Armageddon.

### Revelation 12:13-17

*Now when the dragon saw that he had been cast to the earth, he persecuted the woman who gave birth to the male Child. But the woman was given two wings of a great eagle, that she might fly into the wilderness to her place, where she is nourished for a time and times and half a time, from the presence of the serpent. So the serpent spewed water out of his mouth like a flood after the woman, that he might cause her to be carried away by the flood. But the earth helped the woman, and the earth opened its mouth and swallowed up the flood which the dragon had spewed out of his mouth. And the dragon was enraged with the woman, and he went to make war with the rest of her offspring, who keep the command-ments of God and have the testimony of Jesus Christ.*

The war between the King of the North and the King of the South at the time of the end could be classified as a civil conflict between the two segments of the antichrist's kingdom.

The root of the conflict is related to a difference in religious views and gods. The Muslim nations of the King of the South, will not be that receptive to taking the mark of the beast that Antiochus Epiphanes will be forcing upon the world, nor in recognizing a god that is not Allah. The King of the South will have to give in when he loses the war, because it says he will give his power to the beast, but in doing so he will achieve his goal to wipe out Israel, a goal that is in the minds of the Muslim nations today. This is also the goal of the dragon. The eight horns will encourage the harlot to participate in the battle at Armageddon with this common goal in mind. The eight are the remnant of the ten; the seven remaining after three are uprooted, plus the false prophet, numbering eight in total.

---

**POINT OF INTEREST**
Judgment of Babylon the Great &
**The Marriage of the Lamb**

All of the components of the kingdom of the Antichrist are summed up by God as beginning in Babylon and eventually culminating in the woman with the name of *"Mystery, Babylon the Great, the Mother of Harlots and the Abominations of the Earth"*. God referred to this whole historical and future system as a great city, one that He will specifically judge and destroy at the judgment of Babylon the Great.

*Revelation 18:10*: *"standing at a distance for fear of her torment, saying, 'Alas, alas, that great city Babylon, that mighty city! For in one hour your judgment has come."*

God's judgment immediately prior to the battle at Armageddon will destroy every nature of world systems developed by man. Following this judgment on earth, God will have a wedding ceremony in heaven, the Marriage of the Lamb. This is when Christ, the groom, will be married to His bride, the Church.

*Revelation 19:9*: *" Then he said to me, "Write: 'Blessed are those who are called to the marriage supper of the Lamb!'" And he said to me, "These are the true sayings of God.""*

We know this event also occurs prior to the battle at Armageddon, because every believer will be clothed in white raiment (robes) riding on white horses and will follow Christ when He comes to fight at Armageddon.

*Revelation 19:14*: *" And the armies in heaven, clothed in fine linen, white and clean, followed Him on white horses."*

**Revelation 17:16-18**

*And the ten horns which you saw on the beast, these will hate the harlot, make her desolate and naked, eat her flesh and burn her with fire. For God has put it into their hearts to fulfill His purpose, to be of one mind, and to give their kingdom to the beast, until the words of God are fulfilled. And the woman whom you saw is that great city which reigns over the kings of the earth."*

God will destroy the antichrist's kingdom at the battle at Armageddon.

Five of the seven kings and their respective kingdoms *have fallen, one is, and the other has not yet come.*

**Revelation 17:10**

*There are also seven kings. Five have fallen, one is, and the other has not yet come. And when he comes, he must continue a short time.*

The five fallen would have to be historical kings and kingdoms. From the vision God gave to Nebuchadnezzar we know that Babylon, Media-Persia, Greece, and Rome are kingdoms that will be destroyed by the stone cut without hand (Christ) who will smite the image on its feet of clay and iron (antichrist's kingdom) and shatter the image. This event will be the battle at Armageddon.

**Daniel 2:44-55**

*And in the days of these kings the God of heaven will set up a kingdom which shall never be destroyed; and the kingdom shall not be left to other people; it shall break in pieces and consume all these kingdoms, and it shall stand forever. Inasmuch as you saw that the stone was cut out of the mountain without hands, and that it broke in pieces the iron, the bronze, the clay, the silver, and the gold—the great God has made known to the king what will come to pass after this. The dream is certain, and its terpretation is sure.*

Antiochus Epiphanes, the Syrian ruler will also be destroyed in this battle.

## Daniel 7: 11

*I watched then because of the sound of the pompous words which the horn was speaking; I watched till the beast was slain, and its body destroyed and given to the burning flame.*

With this information the five fallen are identified as the present-day nations of Iraq, Iran, Greece, Syria, and Italy. The Roman Empire of Italy included many nations of Europe in the two legs of iron, being the Eastern and Western divisions of the empire. These nations are now part of the European Union (EU). The *"one is"* kingdom is the nation that John was living in when he wrote the book of Revelation. John was in Turkey and, therefore, Turkey will be the sixth head. The seventh head is the one

**POINT OF INTEREST**
**The Antichrist, The European Union, and the Identity of the Components**

The first Antichrist has not been identified in scripture, however, his kingdom is the beast that looks like a leopard with feet of a bear and the mouth of a lion.

*Revelation 13:2: "Now the beast which I saw was like a leopard, his feet were like the feet of a bear, and his mouth like the mouth of a lion. The dragon gave him his power, his throne, and great authority."*

As mentioned previously the leader and the kingdom are one and the same. The leopard was the kingdom of Greece.

*Daniel 7:6: ""After this I looked, and there was another, like a leopard, which had on its back four wings of a bird. The beast also had four heads, and dominion was given to it. "*

The leader, therefore, will be a Greek citizen. The first antichrist has a power base that allows him to be at war and control all nations. He is a king who proclaims to be a god his forefathers never knew. This precludes him from being a Muslim, since Allah is their god.

Four of his partners under covenant are Muslim nations; for him to be the great pretentious leader of an all-powerful kingdom, reality suggests that he will require the backing of a substantial financial and industrial organization in the general area. His kingdom develops from the fourth kingdom, the Roman Empire, whose nations are now part of the European Union (EU). A Greek citizen would be part of the EU and would readily receive the support of his cohort Antiochus Epiphanes, who also was a Greek-Syrian citizen, one that honored Greek culture. The EU will provide the support the antichrist will need and vice versa.

that has not yet come, the antichrist. The seven heads are joined by the ten horns near the middle of the tribulation period.

### Revelation 17:12-18

*"The ten horns which you saw are ten kings who have received no kingdom as yet, but they receive authority for one hour as kings with the beast. These are of one mind, and they will give their power and authority to the beast. These will make war with the Lamb, and the Lamb will overcome them, for He is Lord of lords and King of kings; and those who are with Him are called, chosen, and faithful." Then he said to me, "The waters which you saw, where the harlot sits, are peoples, multitudes, nations, and tongues. And the ten horns which you saw on the beast, these will hate the harlot, make her desolate and naked, eat her flesh and burn her with fire. For God has put it into their hearts to fulfill His purpose, to be of one mind, and to give their kingdom to the beast, until the words of God are fulfilled. And the woman whom you saw is that great city which reigns over the kings of the earth."*

The ten horns (eight after the false prophet uproots three) are synonymous with the King of the South (Daniel 11:40). Some of the nations of the King of the South are identified in Psalm 83.

The above information is illustrated on the following chart, which also shows the time frame of the tribulation period covering the rule of the antichrist and false prophet.

## Future Kingdom of Antichrist and False Prophet Empowered by Satan

| First 3 ½ Years – The Antichrist | Second 3 ½ - The False Prophet | 75 Days |
|---|---|---|
| Individual: Unknown | Individual: Antiochus Epiphanes | Jacob's Time of Trouble |
| Kingdom: Beast with Seven Heads and Ten Horns | | |

**First Six Seals of Scroll**

Seven heads are seven nations under covenant with antichrist. This power base is the great harlot.

| | | |
|---|---|---|
| Babylon | □ | Iraq |
| Media-Persia | □ | Iran |
| Greece | □ | Greece |
| { Syria / Antiochus Epiphanes } | □ | Syria |
| Rome | □ | Italy |
| Asia | □ | Turkey |
| Great Harlot | □ | Antichrist's Kingdom |

**Mid-Tribulation**

God's Day of Wrath
Seventh Seal of Scroll Broken
Seven Trumpets and Seven Bowls of Wrath

Note: The seven heads are the kingdoms of Nebuchadnezzar's vision that will be destroyed by the stone cut without hand (Christ) at Armageddon. The ten toes get struck and are included in this destruction.

Note: The ten horns are the nations of the King of the South and hate the harlot (seven heads), King of the North. They will give their power to the antichrist.

Note: Iran will be ten Muslim nations of the King of the South, mixing with clay, which are Satan's fallen angels. The False Prophet from the Great Harlot, the seven nations under one covenant, will uproot three of these kings when the King of the North defeats the King of the South. The ten horns will be forced to give their kingdoms and power to the Great Harlot (King of the North).

Ten horns are mid-east nations close to Israel who will each have a king and will rule for one hour with the False Prophet. Three will be uprooted by the False Prophet.

# 7: Judgments

God is in control of all events, which will take place at His appointed times. There are several judgments that will take place at different times and for specific reasons. The judgment seat of Christ, judgment of Babylon the Great, judgment of those who did not take the mark of the beast, and judgment of nations take place about the time of the battle at Armageddon.

## Judgment Seat of Christ

The first judgment, the judgment seat of Christ, will be for believers, who will not be judged for eternal life, but will be judged for the things they have done in the spirit and in good faith.

### John 5:22
*For the Father judges no one, but has committed all judgment to the Son...*

### II Timothy 4:1
*I charge you therefore before God and the Lord Jesus Christ, who will judge the living and the dead at His appearing and His kingdom...*

### II Corinthians 5:9-10
*Therefore we make it our aim, whether present or absent, to be well pleasing to Him. For we must all appear before the judgment seat of Christ, that each one may receive the things*

*done in the body, according to what he has done, whether good or bad.*

## I Corinthians 3:12-15

*Now if anyone builds on this foundation with gold, silver, precious stones, wood, hay, straw, each one's work will become clear; for the Day will declare it, because it will be revealed by fire; and the fire will test each one's work, of what sort it is. If anyone's work which he has built on it endures, he will receive a reward. If anyone's work is burned, he will suffer loss; but he himself will be saved, yet so as through fire.*

**POINT OF INTEREST**
Christ's Judgment

The accuracy of God's word is again revealed. Christ will judge the living and the dead at His appearing, at the time of entering His kingdom.

*I Thessalonians 4:16-18: And the dead in Christ will rise first. Then we who are alive and remain shall be caught up together with them in the clouds to meet the Lord in the air...*

At the time when the Church meets Christ in the air, both the *dead* and the *living* will be then be living and will go to receive their rewards at the judgment seat of Christ, an event that occurs in heaven. The last part of II Timothy 4 refers to Christ's judgment for those He allows to go into His kingdom at the time believers go into the millennium.

*Revelation 20:4: And I saw thrones, and they sat on them, and judgment was committed to them. Then I saw the souls of those who had been beheaded for their witness to Jesus and for the word of God, who had not worshiped the beast or his image, and had not received his mark on their foreheads or on their hands. And they lived and reigned with Christ for a thousand years.*

The judgment which occurs at the time He establishes His kingdom will include the judgment of those who did not take the mark of the beast and those nations that Christ will be considering as sheep nations. This judgment will take place on earth at Christ's second coming. It is my interpretation that the judgments will take place during the first 30 days of the time, times, and a half time period, near the end of the tribulation period.

## Judgment of Babylon the Great

This judgement will take place after the tribulation period, during the 75-day period, while the angel sent from God is preaching the everlasting gospel to those on earth. It is a judgment of the man-made system of corruptness. This system is referred to by God as *the great city*. The system began as far back in time as the Tower of Babel in Babylon and continued its development into the kingdom of the antichrist, *the Great Harlot*.

**See Also:**

❑ *Point of Interest in Chapter 5: Israel in History*

**Revelation 14:6**
*Then I saw another angel flying in the midst of heaven, having the everlasting gospel to preach to those who dwell on the earth—to every nation, tribe, tongue, and people—*

This last message from God is given at the time of His judgment of Babylon, who brought corruption on all nations. This judgment occurs with the proclamation of the second angel, during the second 30-day period of Jacob's time of trouble, while the false prophet is enforcing the mark of the beast.

**Revelation 14:8**
*And another angel followed, saying, "Babylon is fallen, is fallen, that great city, because she has made all nations drink of the wine of the wrath of her fornication."*

Then the third angel issues a warning for people not to take the mark of the beast.

**Revelation 14:9, 10**
*Then a third angel followed them, saying with a loud voice, "If anyone worships the beast and his image, and receives his mark on his forehead or on his hand, he himself shall also drink of the wine of the wrath of God, which is poured out full strength into the cup of His indignation. He shall be tormented with fire and brimstone in the presence of the holy angels and in the presence of the Lamb.*

## Judgment of Those Who Do Not Take the Mark of the Beast

This judgment is for the people who did not take the mark of the beast. They will be allowed to enter the millennium to reign with Christ for 1000 years.

### Revelation 20:4
*And I saw thrones, and they sat on them, and judgment was committed to them. Then I saw the souls of those who had been beheaded for their witness to Jesus and for the word of God, who had not worshiped the beast or his image, and had not received his mark on their foreheads or on their hands. And they lived and reigned with Christ for a thousand years.*

## Judgment of Nations

Christ, at His second coming, after the tribulation and immediately after the battle at Armageddon, will conduct the judgment. He will separate the nations into goat and sheep nations.

### Matthew 25:31-46
*"When the Son of Man comes in His glory, and all the holy angels with Him, then He will sit on the throne of His glory. All the nations will be gathered before Him, and He will separate them one from another, as a shepherd divides his sheep from the goats. And He will set the sheep on His right hand, but the goats on the left. Then the King will say to those on His right hand, 'Come, you blessed of My Father, inherit the kingdom prepared for you from the foundation of the world: for I was hungry and you gave Me food; I was thirsty and you gave Me drink; I was a stranger and you took Me in; I was naked and you clothed Me; I was sick and you visited Me; I was in prison and you came to Me.' Then the righteous will answer Him, saying, 'Lord, when did we see You hungry and feed You, or thirsty and give You drink? When did we see You a stranger and take You in, or naked and clothe You? Or*

*when did we see You sick, or in prison, and come to You?'
And the King will answer and say to them, 'Assuredly, I say
to you, inasmuch as you did it to one of the least of these My
brethren, you did it to Me.' Then He will also say to those on
the left hand, 'Depart from Me, you cursed, into the everlasting fire prepared for the devil and his angels: for I was
hungry and you gave Me no food; I was thirsty and you gave
Me no drink; I was a stranger and you did not take Me in,
naked and you did not clothe Me, sick and in prison and you
did not visit Me.' Then they also will answer Him, saying,
'Lord, when did we see You hungry or thirsty or a stranger
or naked or sick or in prison, and did not minister to You?'
Then He will answer them, saying, 'Assuredly, I say to you,
inasmuch as you did not do it to one of the least of these, you
did not do it to Me.' And these will go away into everlasting
punishment, but the righteous into eternal life.*

Because Christ is sitting on His throne, one would conclude the
judgment will take place at the time of entering His kingdom (the
millennium).

The judgment will be for all nations, some of which were wiped
out or partially so in the battle at Armageddon.

### Zechariah 14: 16-17

*And it shall come to pass that everyone who is left of all
the nations which came against Jerusalem shall go up from
year to year to worship the King, the Lord of hosts, and to
keep the Feast of Tabernacles. And it shall be that whichever
of the families of the earth do not come up to Jerusalem to
worship the King, the Lord of hosts, on them there will be
no rain.*

Sheep nations will be allowed to go into the millennium and
the goat nations will go to destruction. The judgement of nations
is different from the judgment of individual persons. Even though
nations are composed of individual persons, the policies and actions
of the nations can be different than that of the people. Most nations

have a mixture of people, e.g. believers and unbelievers. Christ will divide the nations on their course of action whether they are of good deeds or evil deeds, particularly on how nations treated Israel. The nations that helped other nations when they were in need and that lived by peaceful standards will be allowed to be sheep nations. Those that were evil, lived by the sword and immorality will be goat nations. When it comes to individuals they will either be believers or unbelievers, and face the representative judgements. Some gentile nations will be allowed to go into the millennium.

## Great White Throne of Judgment

After the thousand years have expired, and the battle of Gog and Magog is over, we see the great white throne of judgment for unbelievers. People will be in the second major resurrection, which brings them from the sea, death, and Hades to this judgment. In this judgment the books are opened and the Book of Life will be looked at as well. They will be judged for their works that are written in the books and anyone not found written in the Book of Life will be cast into the lake of fire, which is the second death. This will be eternal separation from God.

### Revelation 20: 11-15
*Then I saw a great white throne and Him who sat on it, from whose face the earth and the heaven fled away. And there was found no place for them. And I saw the dead, small and great, standing before God, and books were opened. And another book was opened, which is the Book of Life. And the dead were judged according to their works, by the things which were written in the books. The sea gave up the dead who were in it, and Death and Hades delivered up the dead who were in them. And they were judged, each one according to his works. Then Death and Hades were cast into the lake of fire. This is the second death. And anyone not found written in the Book of Life was cast into the lake of fire.*

Please note the fact there will be records, and *books were opened, and another book was opened, which is the Book of Life.*

Time of Occurrence and Sequence of Closing Events Prior to the Millennium

| Event | Time of Occurrence | Announced or Conducted By | Punishment/Consequence | Scripture Reference |
|---|---|---|---|---|
| Preaching Everlasting Gospel | Christ on Mount Zion with 144,000 | Angel | | Revelation 13:6-7 |
| Bowl Judgments | Prior to Judgment of Babylon | Seven angels | Refer to Revelation 16 | Revelation 16 |
| Judgment of Babylon | Prior to the battle at Armageddon, and following the preaching of everlasting gospel. Prior to enforcement of taking mark of the beast. | Announced by angel, conducted by God. | Total destruction | Revelation 13:8<br>Revelation 18:8 |
| Warning not to take the mark of the beast. | During 75-day period | Angel | Torment of fire and brimstone forever | Revelation 14:9-11 |
| Reaping the earth's harvest | Prior to Armageddon | Announced by Angel, conducted by Christ. | No punishment, but permission to enter millennium | Revelation 14: 14-16 |
| Battle at Armageddon | Closing at the end | Christ at His second coming | Destruction of antichrist, false prophet, and kingdom | Revelation 19:11-21 |
| Judgment of People who did not take the mark of the beast, but were martyrs. | After Armageddon. | Elders | No punishment, permission to enter millennium. | Revelation 20:4-6 |
| Judgment of Nations | When Christ is sitting on His throne and is establishing His kingdom. | Christ | Goat nations go to everlasting punishment. | Matthew 25:31-46 |

# 8: Millennium

The primary purpose for the millennium is for God to show to the nations that He is Lord. Israel has profaned the Lord's name wherever they have existed. God will cleanse them, and put a new spirit in them, and bless them as a nation, as proof to all other nations that He is Lord, He is truth and He will honor all of His covenants. He will make a new covenant with Israel at the time when they enter their kingdom.

### Ezekiel 36:22, 23

*Therefore say to the house of Israel, 'Thus says the Lord God: "I do not do this for your sake, O house of Israel, but for My holy name's sake, which you have profaned among the nations wherever you went. And I will sanctify My great name, which has been profaned among the nations, which you have profaned in their midst; and the nations shall know that I am the Lord," says the Lord God, "when I am hallowed in you before their eyes.*

### Jeremiah 31:31-34

*"Behold, the days are coming, says the LORD, when I will make a new covenant with the house of Israel and with the house of Judah— not according to the covenant that I made with their fathers in the day that I took them by the hand to lead them out of the land of Egypt, My covenant which they broke, though I was a husband to them,[a] says the LORD. But this is the covenant that I will make with the house of Israel*

*after those days, says the LORD: I will put My law in their minds, and write it on their hearts; and I will be their God, and they shall be My people. No more shall every man teach his neighbor, and every man his brother, saying, 'Know the LORD,' for they all shall know Me, from the least of them to the greatest of them, says the LORD. For I will forgive their iniquity, and their sin I will remember no more."*

## The Covenant

### Ezekiel 20:5-6

*Say to them, 'Thus says the Lord God: "On the day when I chose Israel and raised My hand in an oath to the descendants of the house of Jacob, and made Myself known to them in the land of Egypt, I raised My hand in an oath to them, saying, 'I am the Lord your God.' On that day I raised My hand in an oath to them, to bring them out of the land of Egypt into a land that I had searched out for them, 'flowing with milk and honey,' the glory of all lands.*

### Isaiah 34:17

*He has cast the lot for them, and His hand has divided it among them with a measuring line. They shall possess it forever; from generation to generation they shall dwell in it.*

The land will be divided amongst the twelve tribes of Israel according to Ezekiel 48.

The millennium is the beginning of the kingdom which Israel has been looking for throughout its existence. The kingdom will be in the land that was promised to Abraham, Isaac, and Jacob, and it will be an everlasting kingdom. God will establish the kingdom at His appointed time, when Christ will return to the earth at His second coming, to conduct the judgment of nations, fight the battle at Armageddon, and establish the kingdom. The judgment of nations and the battle at Armageddon are events that allow Christ to begin

His rule with the rod of iron, to ensure peace continues until Satan's release from the pit.

During the millennium Israel will be educated in spiritual matters. Israel will be become a light to the Gentiles, who are the sheep nations from the judgment of nations, that were allowed to go into the millennium.

### Jeremiah 3:15

*And I will give you shepherds according to My heart, who will feed you with knowledge and understanding.*

### Jeremiah 31:34

*No more shall every man teach his neighbor, and every man his brother, saying, 'Know the Lord,' for they all shall know Me, from the least of them to the greatest of them, says the Lord. For I will forgive their iniquity, and their sin I will remember no more.*

### Isaiah 49:6

*Indeed He says, 'It is too small a thing that You should be My Servant To raise up the tribes of Jacob, And to restore the preserved ones of Israel; I will also give You as a light to the Gentiles, That You should be My salvation to the ends of the earth.'*

David will be Israel's king during the millennium.

### Ezekiel 37:24

*David My servant shall be king over them, and they shall all have one shepherd; they shall also walk in My judgments and observe My statutes, and do them.*

Note that they will be living under the laws of the temple. These laws are different from the laws God gave to Moses on Mt. Sinai. There will also be a millennial temple, as described in Ezekiel 40, 41, 42, 43, and 44.

Christ will be in charge of this kingdom because He is the King of Kings and Lord of Lords.

### Revelation 19:16
*And He has on His robe and on His thigh a name written: King Of Kings And Lord Of Lords.*

He is the one who establishes the kingdom and will rule it with a rod of iron.
There will be nations all around Israel.

### Ezekiel 36:36
*Then the nations which are left all around you shall know that I, the Lord, have rebuilt the ruined places and planted what was desolate. I, the Lord, have spoken it, and I will do it.*

### Isaiah 60:3, 4
*The Gentiles shall come to your light, and kings to the brightness of your rising. Lift up your eyes all around, and see: They all gather together, they come to you; your sons shall come from afar, and your daughters shall be nursed at your side.*

### Zechariah 2:11
*Many nations shall be joined to the Lord in that day, and they shall become My people. And I will dwell in your midst. Then you will know that the Lord of hosts has sent Me to you.*

### Isaiah 60:10-12
*The sons of foreigners shall build up your walls, and their kings shall minister to you; for in My wrath I struck you, but in My favour I have had mercy on you. Therefore your gates shall be open continually; they shall not be shut day or night, that men may bring to you the wealth of the Gentiles, and their kings in procession. For the nation and kingdom*

*which will not serve you shall perish, and those nations shall be utterly ruined.*

We can see from these words that there will be many unsaved nations in the earth and this has to be the case because at the end of the millennium Satan will be released from his prison and will go out to deceive the nations.

### Revelation 20:7, 8
*Now when the thousand years have expired, Satan will be released from his prison and will go out to deceive the nations which are in the four corners of the earth, Gog and Magog, to gather them together to battle, whose number is as the sand of the sea.*

It is important to note, God will only fight one battle of Gog and Magog, and this will be at the end of the millennium. The conditions that Israel will be living under are described in Ezekiel 38. Israel will be living in the promised land, in peace, with unwalled villages. There is no doubt that this is Israel in the millennium and that the battle will take place at the end of the millennium as stated in Revelation. This battle is fought by God.

People who will enter the millennium are categorized as follows:

1. Jacob's descendents
2. People who did not take the mark of the beast
3. Sheep nations
4. Dry bones of Ezekiel 37
5. Re-gathered Israelites

1. Jacob's Descendents:
The 144,000 servants of God will be sealed after the sixth seal is broken and the day of God's wrath is about to commence.

**Revelation 6:17**
*For the great day of His wrath has come, and who is able to stand?"*

**Revelation 7:1-8**
*After these things I saw four angels standing at the four corners of the earth, holding the four winds of the earth, that the wind should not blow on the earth, on the sea, or on any tree. Then I saw another angel ascending from the east, having the seal of the living God. And he cried with a loud voice to the four angels to whom it was granted to harm the earth and the sea, saying, "Do not harm the earth, the sea, or the trees till we have sealed the servants of our God on their foreheads." And I heard the number of those who were sealed. One hundred and forty-four thousand of all the tribes of the children of Israel were sealed: of the tribe of Judah twelve thousand were sealed; of the tribe of Reuben twelve thousand were sealed; of the tribe of Gad twelve thousand were sealed; of the tribe of Asher twelve thousand were sealed; of the tribe of Naphtali twelve thousand were sealed; of the tribe of Manasseh twelve thousand were sealed; of the tribe of Simeon twelve thousand were sealed; of the tribe of Levi twelve thousand were sealed; of the tribe of Issachar twelve thousand were sealed of the tribe of Zebulun twelve thousand were sealed; of the tribe of Joseph twelve thousand were sealed; of the tribe of Benjamin twelve thousand were sealed.*

It is evident that the 144,000 will be going through the second half of the tribulation period because God has sealed them in their foreheads to protect them from the events of His wrath. The 144,000 are with Christ on Mount Zion near the end of the tribulation period and are claimed to be first fruits to God. We know they will enter the millennium because the promised land is divided amongst them and their forefathers during the millennium.

**See Also:**

❑ *The Sealing of the 144,000 in our discussion of Revelation Chapter 7.*

**Ezekiel 47:21-23**
*"Thus you shall divide this land among yourselves according to the tribes of Israel. It shall be that you will divide it by lot as an inheritance for yourselves, and for the strangers who dwell among you and who bear children among you. They shall be to you as native-born among the children of Israel; they shall have an inheritance with you among the tribes of Israel. And it shall be that in whatever tribe the stranger dwells, there you shall give him his inheritance," says the Lord God.*

The division of lands will follow God's rules for inheritance.

**Ezekiel 46:17**
*But if he gives a gift of some of his inheritance to one of his servants, it shall be his until the year of liberty, after which it shall return to the prince. But his inheritance shall belong to his sons; it shall become theirs.*

The word *liberty* in the above verse may be interpreted *every 50th year* as according to Leviticus 25.

**Leviticus 25:10**
*And you shall consecrate the fiftieth year, and proclaim liberty throughout all the land to all its inhabitants. It shall be a Jubilee for you; and each of you shall return to his possession, and each of you shall return to his family.*

Nearly all of the scriptures relating to the millennium on this earth, indicate Israel will be living under the law of the temple, they will have been cleansed and will not worship idols any longer, but will honour God and keep His statutes.

2. People Who Did Not Take the Mark of the Beast

The people who endured to the end by being martyrs because they did not worship the beast and take the mark of the beast, will be resurrected and allowed to go into the millennium.

### Revelation 20:4-6

*And I saw thrones, and they sat on them, and judgment was committed to them. Then I saw the souls of those who had been beheaded for their witness to Jesus and for the word of God, who had not worshiped the beast or his image, and had not received his mark on their foreheads or on their hands. And they lived and reigned with Christ for a thousand years. But the rest of the dead did not live again until the thousand years were finished. This is the first resurrection. Blessed and holy is he who has part in the first resurrection. Over such the second death has no power, but they shall be priests of God and of Christ, and shall reign with Him a thousand years.*

3. The Sheep Nations

The nations that extended help to Israel and any other needy nations, will be allowed to go into the millennium. Christ will decide who are sheep nations at the judgment of nations that He will conduct.

### Matthew 25:31-46

*"When the Son of Man comes in His glory, and all the holy angels with Him, then He will sit on the throne of His glory. All the nations will be gathered before Him, and He will separate them one from another, as a shepherd divides his sheep from the goats. And He will set the sheep on His right hand, but the goats on the left. Then the King will say to those on His right hand, 'Come, you blessed of My Father, inherit the kingdom prepared for you from the foundation of the world: for I was hungry and you gave Me food; I was thirsty and you gave Me drink; I was a stranger and you took Me in; I was naked and you clothed Me; I was sick and you visited*

*Me; I was in prison and you came to Me.' Then the righteous will answer Him, saying, 'Lord, when did we see You hungry and feed You, or thirsty and give You drink? When did we see You a stranger and take You in, or naked and clothe You? Or when did we see You sick, or in prison, and come to You?' And the King will answer and say to them, 'Assuredly, I say to you, inasmuch as you did it to one of the least of these My brethren, you did it to Me.' Then He will also say to those on the left hand, 'Depart from Me, you cursed, into the everlasting fire prepared for the devil and his angels: for I was hungry and you gave Me no food; I was thirsty and you gave Me no drink; I was a stranger and you did not take Me in, naked and you did not clothe Me, sick and in prison and you did not visit Me.' Then they also will answer Him, saying, 'Lord, when did we see You hungry or thirsty or a stranger or naked or sick or in prison, and did not minister to You?' Then He will answer them, saying, 'Assuredly, I say to you, inasmuch as you did not do it to one of the least of these, you did not do it to Me.' And these will go away into everlasting punishment, but the righteous into eternal life."*

4.  Dry Bones of Ezekiel 37

The vision of dry bones coming to life was given to Ezekiel. The whole house of Israel who were faithful to God will be resurrected from their graves and placed in their promised land. The tribes will be united into one kingdom with David as their king. God will cleanse them and make them forget the places where they have sinned.

**Ezekiel 37:4-14**

*Again He said to me, "Prophesy to these bones, and say to them, 'O dry bones, hear the word of the LORD! Thus says the Lord GOD to these bones: "Surely I will cause breath to enter into you, and you shall live. I will put sinews on you and bring flesh upon you, cover you with skin and put breath in you; and you shall live. Then you shall know that I am the LORD."'" So I prophesied as I was commanded; and as I prophesied, there was a noise, and suddenly a rattling; and the bones came together, bone to bone. Indeed, as I looked, the sinews and the flesh came upon them, and the skin covered them over; but there was no breath in them. Also He said to me, "Prophesy to the breath, prophesy, son of man, and say to the breath, 'Thus says the Lord GOD: "Come from the four winds, O breath, and breathe on these slain, that they may live."'" So I prophesied as He commanded me, and breath came into them, and they lived, and stood upon their feet, an exceedingly great army. Then He said to me, "Son of man, these bones are the whole house of Israel. They indeed say, 'Our bones are dry, our hope is lost, and we ourselves are cut off!' Therefore prophesy and say to them, 'Thus says the Lord GOD: "Behold, O My people, I will open your graves and cause you to come up from your graves, and bring you into the land of Israel. Then you shall know that I am the LORD, when I have opened your graves, O My people, and brought you up from your graves. I will put My Spirit in you, and you shall live, and I will place you in your own land. Then you shall know that I, the LORD, have spoken it and performed it," says the LORD.'"*

5. Re-Gathered Israelites

Israelites who have been scattered world-wide will be re-gathered to go into the promised land.

### Ezekiel 37:21-28

*"Then say to them, 'Thus says the Lord GOD: "Surely I will take the children of Israel from among the nations, wherever they have gone, and will gather them from every side and bring them into their own land; and I will make them one nation in the land, on the mountains of Israel; and one king shall be king over them all; they shall no longer be two nations, nor shall they ever be divided into two kingdoms again. They shall not defile themselves anymore with their idols, nor with their detestable things, nor with any of their transgressions; but I will deliver them from all their dwelling places in which they have sinned, and will cleanse*

*them. Then they shall be My people, and I will be their God. "David My servant shall be king over them, and they shall all have one shepherd; they shall also walk in My judgments and observe My statutes, and do them. Then they shall dwell in the land that I have given to Jacob My servant, where your fathers dwelt; and they shall dwell there, they, their children, and their children's children, forever; and My servant David shall be their prince forever. Moreover I will make a covenant of peace with them, and it shall be an everlasting covenant with them; I will establish them and multiply them, and I will set My sanctuary in their midst forevermore. My tabernacle also shall be with them; indeed I will be their God, and they shall be My people. The nations also will know that I, the LORD, sanctify Israel, when My sanctuary is in their midst forevermore."'"*

The size and boundaries of Canaan, the original promised land during the time of Moses, is given in the book of Numbers.

## Numbers 34:1-15

*Then the Lord spoke to Moses, saying, "Command the children of Israel, and say to them: 'When you come into the land of Canaan, this is the land that shall fall to you as an inheritance—the land of Canaan to its boundaries. Your southern border shall be from the Wilderness of Zin along the border of Edom; then your southern border shall extend eastward to the end of the Salt Sea; your border shall turn from the southern side of the Ascent of Akrabbim, continue to Zin, and be on the south of Kadesh Barnea; then it shall go on to Hazar Addar, and continue to Azmon; the border shall turn from Azmon to the Brook of Egypt, and it shall end at the Sea. 'As for the western border, you shall have the Great Sea for a border; this shall be your western border. 'And this shall be your northern border: From the Great Sea you shall mark out your border line to Mount Hor; from Mount Hor you shall mark out your border to the entrance of Hamath; then the direction of the border shall be toward*

*Zedad; the border shall proceed to Ziphron, and it shall end at Hazar Enan. This shall be your northern border. 'You shall mark out your eastern border from Hazar Enan to Shepham; the border shall go down from Shepham to Riblah on the east side of Ain; the border shall go down and reach to the eastern side of the Sea of Chinnereth; the border shall go down along the Jordan, and it shall end at the Salt Sea. This shall be your land with its surrounding boundaries.' "Then Moses commanded the children of Israel, saying: "This is the land which you shall inherit by lot, which the Lord has commanded to give to the nine tribes and to the half-tribe. For the tribe of the children of Reuben according to the house of their fathers, and the tribe of the children of Gad according to the house of their fathers, have received their inheritance; and the half-tribe of Manasseh has received its inheritance. The two tribes and the half-tribe have received their inheritance on this side of the Jordan, across from Jericho eastward, toward the sunrise."*

This land was given to Israel as an inheritance at the time God brought them out of Egypt.

### Numbers 36:7
*So the inheritance of the children of Israel shall not change hands from tribe to tribe, for every one of the children of Israel shall keep the inheritance of the tribe of his fathers.*

If you compare the division of the promised land during the time of Moses with the division of land in Ezekiel's vision of the millennium, you will see they are almost identical.

After the 1000 years of peace, Satan will be released form the bottomless pit.

### Revelation 20:7-9
*Now when the thousand years have expired, Satan will be released from his prison and will go out to deceive the nations which are in the four corners of the earth, Gog and Magog,*

to gather them together to battle, whose number is as the
sand of the sea. They went up on the breadth of the earth and
surrounded the camp of the saints and the beloved city. And
fire came down from God out of heaven and devoured them.

## Battle of Gog and Magog

The last battle to take place on earth is the one fought by God
himself, and is called Gog and Magog. It will virtually destroy
mankind of all nations, whoever was against Israel, and it will take
place at the end of the millennium when Satan will be released from
the bottomless pit. Because all of the nations who went into the
millennium increased immensely in population this will be a big
war.

## Revelation 20:8

*...and will go out to deceive the nations which are in the
four corners of the earth, Gog and Magog, to gather them
together to battle, whose number is as the sand of the sea.*

Some interesting details of this battle are given in Ezekiel 38 &
39.

## Ezekiel 38:8

*After many days you will be visited. In the latter years you
will come into the land of those brought back from the sword
and gathered from many people on the mountains of Israel,
which had long been desolate; they were brought out of the
nations, and now all of them dwell safely.*

There is no doubt when this battle will take place; after the re-
gathering of Israel and when they are dwelling safely under the rule
of Christ, who will rule with the rod of iron. Israel will be dwelling
in unwalled villages and will also have become wealthy because
God blessed them throughout the millennium period.

**Ezekiel 38:11-12**
*You will say, 'I will go up against a land of unwalled villages; I will go to a peaceful people, who dwell safely, all of them dwelling without walls, and having neither bars nor gates'— to take plunder and to take booty, to stretch out your hand against the waste places that are again inhabited, and against a people gathered from the nations, who have acquired livestock and goods, who dwell in the midst of the land.*

The time frame for the battle of Gog and Magog is given in Revelation 20: 7-10.

**Revelation 20:7-10**
*Now when the thousand years have expired, Satan will be released from his prison and will go out to deceive the nations which are in the four corners of the earth, Gog and Magog, to gather them together to battle, whose number is as the sand of the sea. They went up on the breadth of the earth and surrounded the camp of the saints and the beloved city. And fire came down from God out of heaven and devoured them. The devil, who deceived them, was cast into the lake of fire and brimstone where the beast and the false prophet are. And they will be tormented day and night forever and ever.*

The battle of Gog and Magog seems to entail the use of wooden spears, bow and arrows, and javelins, because Israel will make fires with them for seven years.

**Ezekiel 39:9-10**
*"Then those who dwell in the cities of Israel will go out and set on fire and burn the weapons, both the shields and bucklers, the bows and arrows, the javelins and spears; and they will make fires with them for seven years. They will not take wood from the field nor cut down any from the forests, because they will make fires with the weapons; and they will*

*plunder those who plundered them, and pillage those who pillaged them," says the Lord God.*

The weaponry of our day will have been destroyed by God's judgements poured out during the tribulation (judgment of Babylon the Great), and by Christ at the battle at Armageddon. During the millennium Christ will not allow nations to develop weapons of mass destruction because He will rule with a rod of iron and maintain peace for Israel.

It will take Israel seven months to bury the slain.

This battle will be the end of all unbelievers. Those who followed Satan into the battle of Gog and Magog will be killed and will be resurrected to take part in the great white throne of judgement with all unbelievers who died previous to the battle.

### Revelation 20:11-15
*Then I saw a great white throne and Him who sat on it, from whose face the earth and the heaven fled away. And there was found no place for them. And I saw the dead, small and great, standing before God, and books were opened. And another book was opened, which is the Book of Life. And the dead were judged according to their works, by the things which were written in the books. The sea gave up the dead who were in it, and Death and Hades delivered up the dead who were in them. And they were judged, each one according to his works. Then Death and Hades were cast into the lake of fire. This is the second death. And anyone not found written in the Book of Life was cast into the lake of fire.*

After the great white throne of judgement, the first heaven and earth will pass away and the people from the millennial kingdom will be transferred by God into the new earth He will create.

### Revelation 21:1
*Now I saw a new heaven and a new earth, for the first heaven and the first earth had passed away. Also there was no more sea.*

### Isaiah 66:22

*"For as the new heavens and the new earth which I will make shall remain before Me," says the Lord, "So shall your descendants and your name remain."*

New Jerusalem will be coming from heaven to the new earth.

### Revelation 21:10

*And he carried me away in the Spirit to a great and high mountain, and showed me the great city, the holy Jerusalem, descending out of heaven from God…*

### Revelation 21:2-3

*Then I, John, saw the holy city, New Jerusalem, coming down out of heaven from God, prepared as a bride adorned for her husband. And I heard a loud voice from heaven saying, "Behold, the tabernacle of God is with men, and He will dwell with them, and they shall be His people. God Himself will be with them and be their God."*

### Revelation 21:22

*But I saw no temple in it, for the Lord God Almighty and the Lamb are its temple.*

God is the one who will make *New* Jerusalem in heaven and this means He can dwell in this new city on the new earth.

### Acts 7:48-50

*However, the Most High does not dwell in temples made with hands, as the prophet says: 'Heaven is My throne, And earth is My footstool. What house will you build for Me? says the Lord, Or what is the place of My rest? Has My hand not made all these things?'*

# 9: Daniel

The book of Daniel was written approximately 600 B.C. The visions given in Daniel covered the kingdoms of his immediate time and extended into the end-times, including the battle at Armageddon. No one but a God who is omnipotent could so accurately foretell the future events, including the nations that would be involved, the details of the events, and the timeframe of the events. Daniel's ancestry is in Israel, therefore, his writings focus on the life of Israel from Babylon to the time of the end.

To understand the future events of the end-times, we have to have knowledge of Israel's past history, particularly about the nations that had a key part in its bondage. Egypt and Assyria were two nations that held Israel in bondage prior to the four major kingdoms described in the book of Daniel. Egypt and Assyria are nations that will be involved in end-time events as separate, opposing segments; namely as segments of the King of the South and King of the North, who will be part of the antichrist's kingdom. The war between these two kings is described in Daniel 11: 40-45.

# Daniel Chapter 2

King Nebuchadnezzar of Babylon had dreams that were given by God in heaven.

**Daniel 2: 28**
*But there is a God in heaven who reveals secrets, and He has made known to King Nebuchadnezzar what will be in the latter days.*

Daniel was able to tell the king what his dream was and also followed with the interpretation of the dream.

**Daniel 2: 19-25**
*Then the secret was revealed to Daniel in a night vision. So Daniel blessed the God of heaven. Daniel answered and said: Blessed be the name of God forever and ever, for wisdom and might are His. And He changes the times and the seasons; He removes kings and raises up kings; He gives wisdom to the wise and knowledge to those who have understanding. He reveals deep and secret things; He knows what is in darkness, and light dwells in Him. I thank you and praise you, O God of my Fathers; You have given to me wisdom and might, and have made known to us the King's demand.*

Note: God's reference to light versus darkness. Also, that wisdom and might belongs to Him and that He is in control of times and seasons. The lawless one will attempt to change times and law according to Daniel 7:25, but God is in control.

Daniel told the king that he had seen a great image.

**Daniel 2: 32-45**
*This images' head was of fine gold, its chest and arms of silver, its belly and thighs of bronze, its legs of iron and its*

*feet partly of iron and partly of clay. You watched while a stone was cut out without hands,* **which struck the image on its feet of iron and clay,** *and broke them in pieces. Then the iron, the clay, the bronze, the silver, and the gold were crushed together, and became like chaff from the summer threshing floors; the wind carried them away so that no trace of them was found. And the stone that struck the image became a great mountain and filled the whole earth. This is the dream. Now we will tell the interpretation of it before the king. You, O king, are a king of kings. For the God of heaven has given you a kingdom, power, strength, and glory; and wherever the children of men dwell, or the beasts of the field and the birds of the heaven, He has given them into your hand, and has made you ruler over them all—you are this head of gold. But after you shall arise another kingdom inferior to yours; then another, a third kingdom of bronze, which shall rule over all the earth. And the fourth kingdom shall be as strong as iron, inasmuch as iron breaks in pieces and shatters everything; and like iron that crushes, that kingdom will break in pieces and crush all the others. Whereas you saw the feet and toes, partly of potter's clay and partly of iron, the kingdom shall be divided; yet the strength of the iron shall be in it, just as you saw the iron mixed with ceramic clay. And as the toes of the feet were partly of iron and partly of clay, so the kingdom shall be partly strong and partly fragile. As you saw iron mixed with ceramic clay, they will mingle with the seed of men; but they will not adhere to one another, just as iron does not mix with clay. And in the days of these kings the God of heaven will set up a kingdom which shall never be destroyed; and the kingdom shall not be left to other people; it shall break in pieces and consume all these kingdoms, and it shall stand forever. Inasmuch as you saw that the stone was cut out of the mountain without hands, and that it broke in pieces the iron, the bronze, the clay, the silver, and the gold—the great God has made known to the king what will* *come to pass after this. The dream is certain, and its interpretation is sure.*

The first four kingdoms King Nebuchadnezzar saw were the gold, silver, bronze, and iron kingdoms; these being Babylon, Media-Persia, Greece, and Rome, respectively. No mention was made of the rule of Syria under Antiochus Epiphanes, perhaps because his rule was short and he was a king with a kingdom that did not have world-wide control. The rule of Antiochus Epiphanes preceded the major kingdom of Rome.

The *legs of iron* represent the original Roman Empire with western and eastern divisions, covering much of Europe and culminating at Pergamos. The remains of the empire are kingdoms and nations existing today, the most significant development being the recently formed European Union. Nations from the European Union will form the power base of the antichrist's kingdom, when he arises. This last kingdom is referred to as the feet of iron and clay. The iron represents present day kingdoms and nations (beginning from the Roman Empire, as the *One Is* kingdom. These will be united with the clay, which represents Satan and his fallen angels. This will happen in the second half of the tribulation period near the 75-day period (Jacob's *time of trouble*), when the war in heaven breaks out and Satan and his fallen angels are cast to the earth by Michael. The angels that fall to the earth will have to mingle with the seed of men (mankind). They will be following the commands of Satan who is their leader, who also will be commanding the antichrist (false prophet) and his earthly armies. Satan will be persecuting Israel, trying to annihilate them, in this period of time called time, times and half of a time (Jacob's *time of trouble*).

Note: This 75 day period is a distinct period, separate from the second half of the tribulation (last 3 ½ years). The Lord says that if these **days** were not shortened that no life would be spared. If time, times, and half of a time would refer to 3 ½ years, God would likely have said if these years were not shortened, but He said **days**.

Israel will be fleeing into the wilderness when God's day of wrath (the second half of the tribulation period, 1260 days) begins.

## Revelation 12:6

*Then the woman fled into the wilderness, where she has a place prepared by God, that they should feed her there one thousand two hundred and sixty days.*

Note: God did not say time, times, and half of time.

## Revelation 12:7-17

*And war broke out in heaven: Michael and his angels fought with the dragon; and the dragon and his angels fought, but they did not prevail, nor was a place found for them in heaven any longer. So the great dragon was cast out, that serpent of old, called the Devil and Satan, who deceives the whole world; he was cast to the earth, and his angels were cast out with him. Then I heard a loud voice saying in heaven, "Now salvation, and strength, and the kingdom of our God, and the power of His Christ have come, for the accuser of our brethren, who accused them before our God day and night, has been cast down. And they overcame him by the blood of the Lamb and by the word of their testimony, and they did not love their lives to the death. Therefore rejoice, O heavens, and you who dwell in them! Woe to the inhabitants of the earth and the sea! For the devil has come down to you, having great wrath, because he knows that he has a short time." Now when the dragon saw that he had been cast to the earth, he persecuted the woman who gave birth to the male Child. But the woman was given two wings of a great eagle, that she might fly into the wilderness to her place, where she is nourished for a time and times and half a time, from the presence of the serpent. So the serpent spewed water out of his mouth like a flood after the woman, that he might cause her to be carried away by the flood. But the earth helped the woman, and the earth opened its mouth and swallowed up the flood which the dragon had spewed out of his mouth. And the dragon was enraged with the woman, and he went to make war with the rest of her offspring, who keep the commandments of God and have the testimony of Jesus Christ.*

In this passage the war in heaven occurs and Satan and the fallen angels are cast to the earth and Satan will attempt to annihilate Israel. At this time Israel will receive God's help to fly into the wilderness where God will feed her for a time, times, and half of a time. This is the short time Satan will have, namely 75 days, which is time, times, and half of a time.

The kingdom of the feet and toes, partly iron and partly of clay will be the future kingdom of the antichrist. Please note that this kingdom will be partly strong and partly fragile, just as iron does not mix with clay. Also, the comment *"they will mingle with the seed of men"* means that Satan's fallen angels (the clay) will be present during this kingdom and they will be exerting their control with earthly men who are rulers, at that time. The last kingdom Nebuchadnezzar saw was the kingdom that Christ will establish on earth commencing with the millennium and continuing forever.

The stone cut without hand means that God will be involved, wherein the stone is a reference to Christ who will smite the image (the four kings and the kingdom of iron and clay) and destroy it. This will happen when Christ comes from heaven to fight the kings gathered in the valley of Meggido for the battle at Armageddon. We can conclude, therefore, that the five kingdoms of the image will be at this battle.

The clay appears to be Satan and his fallen angels. The angels will mix with men, *not adhere to one another,* but due to Satan's influence and power they will be controlling world affairs and deceiving mankind.

# Daniel Chapters 3 -6

### Daniel Chapter 3
In this chapter the account is given of the fiery furnace and God's protection of Shadrach, Meshach, and Abed-Nego who were unharmed.

### Daniel Chapter 4
King Nebuchadnezzar loses power as a ruler and becomes like an animal. This was directed by God. The conclusion in the chapter gives the account of restoration of his kingdom and his acknowledgement of God.

### Daniel Chapter 5
The *Mene Mene Tekel Upharsin* relates to Belshazzar, who was the son of Nebuchadnezzar. It describes the defeat of the kingdom of Babylon by the Medes and Persians.

### Daniel Chapter 6
We are given the account of Daniel being protected by God and surviving the den of lions.

# Daniel Chapter 7

Daniel's own dream and visions were about the same four kingdoms that Nebuchadnezzar saw, but the kingdoms looked like animals and are called beasts.

### Daniel 7:4
*The first was like a lion, and had eagle's wings. I watched till its wings were plucked off; and it was lifted up from the earth and made to stand on two feet like a man, and a man's heart was given to it.*

In this verse we see the kingdom of Babylon was given to Nebuchadnezzar by God (*had eagles wings*).

### Daniel 2:37
*You, O king, are a king of kings. For the God of heaven has given you a kingdom, power, strength, and glory;*

*Eagle's wings* refers to God's power.

### Exodus 19:4
*You have seen what I did to the Egyptians, and how I bore you on eagles' wings and brought you to Myself.*

*Its wings plucked off* is the account in Daniel 4, where Nebuchadnezzar lost God's support, and *a man's heart was given to it* is the restoration in Daniel 4:36.

### Daniel 7:5
*And suddenly another beast, a second, like a bear. It was raised up on one side, and had three ribs in its mouth between its teeth. And they said thus to it: 'Arise, devour much flesh!'*

The bear is the kingdom that was Media-Persia.

### Daniel 8:20
*The ram which you saw, having the two horns—they are the kings of Media and Persia.*

### Daniel 7:6
*After this I looked, and there was another, like a leopard, which had on its back four wings of a bird. The beast also had four heads, and dominion was given to it.*

The leopard was Greece under Alexander the Great as described in Daniel 8:21.

### Daniel 8:21
*And the male goat is the kingdom of Greece. The large horn that is between its eyes is the first king.*

### Daniel 7: 7- 8
*After this I saw in the night visions, and behold, a fourth beast, dreadful and terrible, exceedingly strong. It had huge iron teeth; it was devouring, breaking in pieces, and trampling the residue with its feet. It was different from all the beasts that were before it, and it had ten horns. I was considering the horns, and there was another horn, a little one, coming up among them, before whom three of the first horns were plucked out by the roots. And there, in this horn, were eyes like the eyes of a man, and a mouth speaking pompous words.*

### Daniel 7:25
*He shall speak pompous words against the Most High, shall persecute the saints of the Most High, and shall intend to change times and law. Then the saints shall be given into his hand for a time and times and half a time.*

The court that will be seated at this time will take away the dominion of the false prophet.

### Daniel 7:26

*But the court shall be seated, and they shall take away his dominion, to consume and destroy it forever.*

### Daniel 7:24-26

*The ten horns are ten kings who shall arise from this kingdom. And another shall rise after them; he shall be different from the first ones, and shall subdue three kings. He shall speak pompous words against the Most High, shall persecute the saints of the Most High, and shall intend to change times and law. Then the saints shall be given into his hand for a time and times and half a time. But the court shall be seated, and they shall take away his dominion, to consume and destroy it forever.*

# Daniel Chapter 8

The vision Daniel had in Chapter 7 was his first, called the Vision by Night. It contained scenes from past time to future end-times, and Daniel was troubled because he could not understand the vision. The vision included the Roman empire of iron, the anti-christ's empire with the ten horns, and the empire Christ will set up as His Kingdom.

The false prophet's rule has two stages, both are prophetic for Daniel. The first stage is during the rule of Antiochus Epiphanes, prior to the Roman kingdom, and the second is when he returns as the false prophet in mid-tribulation. The first stage is described in Daniel 8:23-25.

### Daniel 8:23-25

*And in the latter time of their kingdom, when the transgressors have reached their fullness, a king shall arise, having fierce features, who understands sinister schemes. His power shall be mighty, but not by his own power; he shall destroy fearfully, and shall prosper and thrive; he shall destroy the mighty, and also the holy people. "Through his cunning he shall cause deceit to prosper under his rule; and he shall exalt himself in his heart. he shall destroy many in their prosperity. He shall even rise against the Prince of princes; but he shall be broken without human means.*

Here the vision is given as a Vision of the Evenings, however, when the false prophet returns in the future it is the Vision of the Mornings.

### Daniel 8:25,26

*Through his cunning he shall cause deceit to prosper under his rule; and he shall exalt himself in his heart. He shall destroy many in their prosperity. He shall even rise against the Prince of princes; but he shall be broken without human means. "And the vision of the evenings and mornings which was told is true; therefore seal up the vision, for it refers to many days in the future.*

Daniel 8:1-8 is about the war between Media-Persia and Greece. Daniel informs that he had a second vision, in which Alexander the Great was the main horn that was broken and four kingdoms arise from Alexander's four generals who took over his kingdom.

### Daniel 8:22
*As for the broken horn and the four that stood up in its place, four kingdoms shall arise out of that nation, but not with its power.*

The four kingdoms with less power than Greece arise from the four generals that were part of Alexander's kingdom.

### Daniel 8:23-26
*And in the latter time of their kingdom, when the transgressors have reached their fullness, a king shall arise, having fierce features, who understands sinister schemes. His power shall be mighty, but not by his own power; he shall destroy fearfully, and shall prosper and thrive; he shall destroy the mighty, and also the holy people. Through his cunning he shall cause deceit to prosper under his rule; and he shall exalt himself in his heart. He shall destroy many in their prosperity. He shall even rise against the Prince of Princes; but he shall be broken without human means. And the vision of the evenings and mornings which was told is true; therefore seal up the vision, for it refers to many days in the future."*

Here we see a king (horn) arise from one of Alexander's generals who has given himself to Satan's power (*but not by his own power*) to be cunning and deceitful. He shall rise against the Prince of Princes (Christ) but will be broken without human means by Christ at the battle at Armageddon; as it says many days in the future.

**II Thessalonians 2:6-10**

*And now you know what is restraining, that he may be revealed in his own time. For the mystery of lawlessness is already at work; only He who now restrains will do so until He is taken out of the way. And then the lawless one will be revealed, whom the Lord will consume with the breath of His mouth and destroy with the brightness of His coming. The coming of the lawless one is according to the working of Satan, with all power, signs, and lying wonders, and with all unrighteous deception among those who perish, because they did not receive the love of the truth, that they might be saved.*

The aforementioned little horn comes from the Selucid chain of kings and his name is Antiochus Epiphanes, the eighth king of Syria who reigned from 175 to 164 B.C.

**Daniel 8:11**

*He even exalted himself as high as the Prince of the host; and by him the daily sacrifices were taken away, and the place of His sanctuary was cast down.*

**Daniel 11:31**

*And forces shall be mustered by him, and they shall defile the sanctuary fortress; then they shall take away the daily sacrifices, and place there the abomination of desolation.*

History references tell us that Antiochus Epiphanes sacrificed pigs on the altar and set up his god (Zeus) in the sanctuary.

# Daniel Chapters 9 & 10

### Daniel Chapter 9

Daniel makes his sincere prayer for his people. While he was praying he had a vision, which troubled him. The angel Gabriel came to give Daniel understanding of the vision.

### Daniel 9:24

*Seventy weeks are determined for your people and for your holy city, to finish the transgression, to make an end of sins, to make reconciliation for iniquity, to bring in everlasting righteousness, to seal up vision and prophecy, and to anoint the Most Holy.*

### Daniel 9:25-27

*Know therefore and understand, that from the going forth of the command to restore and build Jerusalem until Messiah the Prince, there shall be seven weeks and sixty-two weeks; the street shall be built again, and the wall, even in troublesome times. And after the sixty-two weeks Messiah shall be cut off, but not for Himself; and the people of the prince who is to come shall destroy the city and the sanctuary. The end of it shall be with a flood, and till the end of the war desolations are determined. Then he shall confirm a covenant with many for one week; but in the middle of the week He shall bring an end to sacrifice and offering. And on the wing of abominations shall be one who makes desolate, even until the consummation, which is determined, is poured out on the desolate.*

In these verses the time frame for 69 of the 70 weeks is given and it goes on to explain the 70th week in verse 27, which will begin with the time that the antichrist comes on the scene with a covenant he will make with many nations. This group of nations will be his power base.

The 70th week is a period of seven years duration and is divided into two periods of three and a half years each. The first three and a half years will be the kingdom of the beast (first antichrist) and the second three and a half year period is when the false prophet (second antichrist) will be in charge. The false prophet is the one who will set up the abomination of desolation for the second time in the tribulation period (70th week).

### Daniel Chapter 10

The vision in Chapter 10 is the greatest vision Daniel received. Daniel knew this vision was given by a glorious-appearing man and recognized the man he saw was divine. In verse 16, Daniel says *"my Lord"*. From verse 1 we see that Daniel understood the vision was a long time coming and he had understanding about some aspects of the vision itself. Remember that Daniel had previously been informed by Gabriel some of the visions were related to the latter days. This vision, however, brought great sorrow to Daniel and took all of his strength from him. The vision of the glory of God made Daniel frail.

John had a similar experience when he encountered the glory of God in a vision. In Revelation 1:17 John says:

### Revelation 1:17
*And when I saw Him, I fell at His feet as dead ….*

After Daniel received this vision, God again sent an angel to provide information on the interpretation. It is interesting to read the comments of the angel, because it shows the angels are working out God's will in controlling the affairs of nations on earth. The vision itself is given in Daniel Chapter 11.

# Daniel Chapter 11

In this chapter Daniel gives us a review of the nations and kings that were seeking control through wars, which often involved family affairs and relationships. His review begins with the war between Media-Persia and Greece. He again refers to Alexander the Great and his four generals from which four kingdoms would arise. The two generals which were of most significance namely, Selucid and Potolemy, were the kingdoms of Syria and Egypt respectively. Potolemy is then referred to as the king of the south, and Selucid the king of the north. The historical wars between the king of the north and the king of the south are described by Daniel and they match the accounts you will find in the history records. In Daniel 11:23-25 we see the first appearance of Antiochus Epiphanes (the little horn). From verse 36-39 we see the antichrist, the first beast, spoken of in Revelation 13. He is the one that blasphemes God and magnifies himself above every God. He is the king of the north. At the time of the end, the king of the south will attack him. The king of the north will win this war and he will establish his headquarters between the seas and the glorious holy mountain. He will come to his end at the battle at Armageddon.

Daniel described the historical battles between the king of the north and the king of the south with sufficient detail that the nations involved can be identified and explained. His account starting in Daniel 11:36 with the future kingdom of the antichrist and continuing to Daniel 11:45 is, however, more difficult to understand. Particularly with the identity of the king of the north and the king of the south who will go to war with each other at the time of the end. The traditional king of the south was Egypt, but this does not seem to be the case in this instance; the words describe Egypt as one who does not escape, but is more of a victim of the war as opposed to an attacking aggressor or instigator. The development of this last war, a war between components of the antichrist's kingdom, will be better understood by reviewing the components of this kingdom.

## See Also:

❑ *Chapter 6 in this book, for information on the kingdom of the antichrist and the above-mentioned war.*

# Daniel Chapter 12

Daniel envisions Michael, the chief angel for the nation of Israel, standing up for Israel during Jacob's time of trouble. This is the time of the war in heaven when Michael and his angels evict Satan and the fallen angels from heaven.

### Revelation 12:7-9

*And war broke out in heaven: Michael and his angels fought with the dragon; and the dragon and his angels fought, but they did not prevail, nor was a place found for them in heaven any longer. So the great dragon was cast out, that serpent of old, called the Devil and Satan, who deceives the whole world; he was cast to the earth, and his angels were cast out with him.*

Now that Satan is cast to the earth Daniel says there will be a time of trouble.

### Daniel 12:1-3

*At that time Michael shall stand up, the great prince who stands watch over the sons of your people; and there shall be a time of trouble, such as never was since there was a nation, even to that time. And at that time your people shall be delivered, every one who is found written in the book. And many of those who sleep in the dust of the earth shall awake, some to everlasting life, some to shame and everlasting contempt. Those who are wise shall shine like the brightness of the firmament, and those who turn many to righteousness like the stars forever and ever.*

Here we have an account of the war in heaven and the time of severe trouble. This starts the 75 day period consisting of 30 days,

30 days, and 15 days, or time, times and ½ of a time known as *Jacob's time of trouble.*

**Daniel 12:7**
*Then I heard the man clothed in linen, who was above the waters of the river, when he held up his right hand and his left hand to heaven, and swore by Him who lives forever, that it shall be for a time, times, and half a time; and when the power of the holy people has been completely shattered, all these things shall be finished.*

We then see that there is a resurrection for the Israelites whose names are in the Book of Life, and they will rise to everlasting life. The Book of Life is God's record that lists the names of all, and notes who will spend eternity with Him, namely, those who have accepted His plan for mankind, discussed previously as the Mystery of God.

**See Also:**

❑ *Chapter 1: God vs. Satan in this book.*

Daniel is told that his people will be delivered during *Jacob's time of trouble*, the 75-day period at the very end of the tribulation, just prior to the battle at Armageddon.

**Daniel 12:1**
*And at that time your people shall be delivered, every one who is found written in the book.*

At this point in time, near the end of the tribulation, the only Jews who will have their name in the Book of Life are those who did not take the mark of the beast and the 144,000 who were sealed. These are the ones that will be delivered. This deliverance is the last harvest that Christ will make prior to the battle at Armageddon.

Further reference to this point in time, the Last Harvest, is found in:

## Revelation 14:14-16

*Then I looked, and behold, a white cloud, and on the cloud sat One like the Son of Man, having on His head a golden crown, and in His hand a sharp sickle. And another angel came out of the temple, crying with a loud voice to Him who sat on the cloud, "Thrust in Your sickle and reap, for the time has come for You to reap, for the harvest of the earth is ripe." So He who sat on the cloud thrust in His sickle on the earth, and the earth was reaped.*

## Revelation 20:4-6

*And I saw thrones, and they sat on them, and judgment was committed to them. Then I saw the souls of those who had been beheaded for their witness to Jesus and for the word of God, who had not worshiped the beast or his image, and had not received his mark on their foreheads or on their hands. And they lived and reigned with Christ for a thousand years. But the rest of the dead did not live again until the thousand years were finished. This is the first resurrection. Blessed and holy is he who has part in the first resurrection. Over such the second death has no power, but they shall be priests of God and of Christ, and shall reign with Him a thousand years.*

## See Also:

❑ *Chapter 10: Revelation, in this book, specifically Revelation Chapter 14, for more information on the last harvest.*

The judgment referred to in Revelation 20:4 above, is for those who did not take the mark of the beast. This is a different and separate judgment from the one that follows the millennium, which is called the great white throne judgment, and is appointed by God for all unbelievers.

**Daniel 12:11-12**

*And from the time that the daily sacrifice is taken away, and the abomination of desolation is set up, there shall be one thousand two hundred and ninety days. Blessed is he who waits, and comes to the one thousand three hundred and thirty-five days.*

In this reference the first 30-day period is added to the 1260 days of the last half of the tribulation, to arrive at 1290 days. The remaining 45 days from the separate75-day period (Jacob's *time of trouble*) are added to 1290 to arrive at 1335 days.

There are specific events that take place in heaven and on earth during the 75-day period, such as, the marriage of the lamb, the judgment seat of Christ, the judgment of Babylon the Great and the judgment of nations. Meanwhile on earth, Satan and his angels and the false prophet are trying to annihilate Israel from the face of the earth. God promises Israel protection and will feed them during the last half of the tribulation period, and during the 75-day period of Jacob's time of trouble.

# 10: Revelation

Everyone who is alive today should familiarize themselves with the contents of the book of Revelation. It is God-given information about the future for mankind. No book that has been written, or ever will be written, can even come close to providing information that is as relevant or important as that given in the Book of Revelation. Only the unwise will not take time to read and have regard for these words, and prepare themselves, their families and loved ones for what lies ahead. If you or your family are those who are left behind when the church is resurrected and taken into heaven, do you know what the conditions will be like on earth and the hardships that you will have to face? If you do not know the answer, you owe it to yourself to read Revelation.

# Reference Terms Used in the book of Revelation

| | | |
|---|---|---|
| 1 | Historical Kingdoms "5 Fallen" Revelation 17:10 | 1. BabylonIraq<br>2. Media-PersiaIran<br>3. GreeceGreece<br>4. SyriaSyria<br>5. RomeRome |
| 2 | Church Age Resurrection & Judgment Seat of Christ | Christ is the head of the Church. When He appears He will resurrect the dead who believed in Him and together with those believers who are alive at His coming. He will transform them into spiritual beings, take them to heaven, and reward them. |
| 3 | Future Kingdom of Satan – antichrist and False Prophet | Satan will empower two men referred to as antichrist and False Prophet. These men will be world rulers of the next kingdom on the earth. Their kingdom is the beast with seven heads and ten horns. |

| | | |
|---|---|---|
| 4 | Sealing 144,000 War in Heaven Resurrection of Martyrs from first half of tribulation period | God seals the 12 tribes of Israel to protect them from His wrath during the second half and the 75 days of tribulation. The martyrs of the first half of tribulation will be resurrected. The war in heaven is Michael against Satan and his fallen angels. Satan is defeated and cast to the earth. |
| | | |
| 5 | God's Day of Wrath Seven Trumpets Two Witnesses Bowl Judgments | God's wrath will be poured out on Satan and his followers during the second half of the tribulation. There will be separate events from the seven trumpets and bowls of wrath. God will also have two witnesses preaching the gospel of the kingdom, and an angel who preaches the everlasting gospel, just prior to the battle at Armageddon. |
| | | |
| 6 | Judgment of Babylon The Great The Mother of Harlots | God will judge the harlot that began with Babylon and climaxes with the kingdom of the antichrist. All martyrs and a multitude in heaven will rejoice when this corrupt *city* is brought to its end. The harlot is the seven heads of the first antichrist. This kingdom of seven nations is called the *great city*. |
| | | |
| 7 | Marriage of the Lamb | Christ will receive his redeemed church as His beloved bride. There will be a great marriage supper in heaven. |
| | | |

| 8 | Battle at Armageddon Satan Bound in Bottomless Pit for 1000 Years | Christ will come back to the earth a second time to fight Satan and the antichrist's armies at Armageddon. The antichrists are thrown into the lake of fire and Satan is bound and placed in the bottomless pit for 1000 years. |
|---|---|---|
|  |  |  |
| 9 | Judgment of Nations Resurrection of Those Who Did Not Receive Mark of the Beast | Christ will conduct judgment of nations. Nations will either be sheep or goats. Goats will be destroyed, sheep will go into millennium. Those who did not take the mark of the beast will be received by Christ at the harvest of the earth, and they will be allowed to go into the millennium. |
|  |  |  |
| 10 | Millennium Israel and Sheep Nations David to be King of Israel | People who did not take the mark of the beast, sheep nations, 144,000 sealed and the nation of Israel who will be re-gathered and those who will be resurrected (Dry Bones of Ezekiel 37) will go into the millennium kingdom. |
|  |  |  |
| 11 | Satan Released Battle of Gog and Magog | After the 1000 years of peace, Satan is released from the bottomless pit and he deceives the nations of the world to do battle with Israel. God will destroy Satan and all his followers at the Battle of Gog and Magog. |
|  |  |  |

| 12 | Great White Throne Judgment | All non-believing dead will be resurrected to face judgment. |
|----|------------------------------|------------------------------------------------------------|
|    |                              |                                                            |
| 13 | Old Earth and Heavens Burned and New Earth and Heavens Created | God will burn the earth and heavens and make a new earth and heavens. |
|    |                              |                                                            |
| 14 | New Jerusalem Comes from Heaven to New Earth "Lamb's Wife" | God's city prepared in heaven for those Israelites who lived through the millennium and will be transferred to the new earth. |
|    |                              |                                                            |
| 15 | River of Life | River that proceeds from God's throne with the water of everlasting life for those in the new heaven. |

# Revelation Chapter 1

### Revelation 1:1
*The Revelation of Jesus Christ, which God gave Him to show His servants—things which must shortly take place.*

Christ is the Son of God, crucified to be a savior, who rose from the dead, who will rule the earth, who is coming again in the clouds. God the Father, authorized Christ to reveal His prophecy to His servants. Christ sent the prophesy by visions through angels to His servant John. John, in the book of Revelation, faithfully recorded all that he witnessed.

### Revelation 1:7
*Behold, He is coming with clouds, and every eye will see Him, even they who pierced Him. And all the tribes of the earth will mourn because of Him. Even so, Amen.*

*For every eye will see Him coming with clouds* implies that every one, dead or alive, will see Him coming, and unbelievers in Sheol and Hades will be awakened to witness this event. The *coming with clouds* is the second coming, but **is not**

---

**POINT OF INTEREST**
The Two Witnesses
John will join Elijah as one of the two witnesses that will proclaim the word of God during the last half of the tribulation period. They will witness for 1260 days, clothed in sackcloth.
***Revelation 11:3,4*** *And I will give power to my two witnesses, and they will prophesy one thousand two hundred and sixty days, clothed in sackcloth. These are the two olive trees and the two lampstands standing before the God.*
**See Also**
*To understand that John is commissioned to be one of the witnesses refer to the discussion of Revelation Chapter 11 (Revelation 11:4-13).*
*The reference for Elijah as one of the two witnesses is Malachi 4:5.*
***Malachi 4:5****: Behold I will send you Elijah the prophet before the coming of the great and dreadful day of the Lord.*

the rapture, although many have previously interpreted it to be the rapture.

At the time of the rapture, Christ appears in the air to meet the believers, but does not physically come to the earth. At His appearance, believers are awakened to rise and meet Christ in the air; this event is the rapture of the Church.

The second coming is when Christ comes to fight the battle at Armageddon, and He will physically be on the earth. Christ's appearing at the time of the rapture and the second coming, are separate events and occur at different times.

In the rapture His appearing is **in** the clouds, to take His church out of the world.

### I Thessalonians 4:16-17

*For the Lord Himself will descend from heaven with a shout, with the voice of an archangel, and with the trumpet of God. And the dead in Christ will rise first. Then we who are alive and remain shall be caught up together with them in the clouds to meet the Lord in the air. And thus we shall always be with the Lord.*

### Revelation 1:16

*He had in His right hand seven stars, out of His mouth went a sharp two-edged sword, and His countenance was like the sun shining in its strength.*

The reference to the sword in His mouth refers to His second coming to fight the battle. This sword is the Word which He will speak and it will be done.

In the second coming, Christ will be coming to judge and make war. Christ instructed John to send His message to the seven angels of the seven churches in Asia. These churches, as listed in Revelation 1:11, are:

The church at:

• Ephasus
• Smyrna

- Pergamos
- Thyatira
- Sardis
- Philadelphia
- Laodicea

These churches were all cities in Turkey, where John had his ministry at the time.

John saw Christ in the midst of seven golden lampstands with seven stars in His hand. The vision of Christ was remarkable, His eyes, feet, voice, hand, two edged sword in His mouth, and His countenance of glory. Christ also made the claim He lives, died, is alive forever more and He has the keys of Hades and of Death. This vision of the sword confirms that it is His second coming to make war, and the mourning confirms it is not a happy event. His appearing during the rapture will be a happy event.

---

**POINT OF INTEREST**

The Timing of the Rapture

The issue of whether the resurrection of the church occurs prior to the tribulation period is still a question many believers enquire about. A sound piece of evidence in providing an answer is obtained by comparing the scene in heaven found in Ezekiel 1, which shows God on the throne surrounded by the four living creatures, to the scene in heaven of Revelation 4 and 5, where God is on the throne surrounded by the four living creatures and twenty-four thrones on which twenty-four elders are seated. In the midst of the elders is a Lamb. The elders sing a new song saying to Christ

" *You are worthy to take the scroll, and to open its seals; You were slain, and have redeemed us to God by Your blood, out of every tribe, tongue, people, and nations.*"

Who did Christ redeem? Believers. The elders are representatives of believers that were redeemed, the church. Remember they are in heaven, when they make the decision that Christ should break the seals of the scroll. After Christ opens the first seal the tribulation period begins, and we have evidence that believers are in heaven prior to the beginning of the tribulation. The elders are worthy ambassadors of the church and are seated on thrones surrounding the throne of God.

---

## Revelation 19:11

*Now I saw heaven opened, and behold, a white horse. And He who sat on him was called Faithful and True, and in righteousness He judges and makes war.*

### Revelation 2:7

*"He who has an ear, let him hear what the Spirit says to the churches. To him who overcomes I will give to eat from the tree of life, which is in the midst of the Paradise of God."*

In all of His messages to the churches in Asia, who will be going through the tribulation period, He says *to him who overcomes I will give.* The words to the churches tie in to the last words given by Christ.

### Revelation 22:7

*"Behold, I am coming quickly! Blessed is he who keeps the words of the prophecy of this book."*

### Revelation 22:12

*"And behold, I am coming quickly, and My reward is with Me, to give to every one according to his work."*

Christ's rewards referred to in verse 12 above, are for the believers who endured the tribulation period, because they kept the words of prophecy given in the book of Revelation.

### Revelation 1:19

*Write the things which you have seen, and the things which are, and the things which will take place after this.*

This was said to John. *The things which you have seen,* refers to the vision of Christ and Christ holding seven stars in His hand and being in the midst of seven lampstands. It also refers to what John knew about the history in the churches where he ministered. *The things which are* refers to the conditions in the seven churches at the time of John, and the things *which will take place after this* are the events given in the book of Revelation beginning with Chapter 4 through to the end of the book of Revelation.

# Revelation Chapters 2 & 3

In the messages to the seven churches Christ reveals separately to each church their historical behaviour (*things you have seen*), what the condition was at John's time (*things which are*), and what the condition will be for the church in the future during the period of tribulation (*things which will take place after this*). In every case Christ identifies himself to each church, as in:

**Revelation 2:8**
*And to the angel of the church in Smyrna write, 'These things says the First and the Last, who was dead, and came to life...*

Christ also lets each church know that He is omnipotent:

**Revelation 2:13**
*I know your works, and where you dwell, where Satan's throne is...*

He then proceeds to discuss their weaknesses and issues warnings on how to correct their behaviour. God's message is the same to all who believe in Him, love Him, honour Him and abide by the principalities of light. Christ knew that He would have His redeemed church in heaven prior to the commencement of the tribulation period.

His messages are also to the churches that will be in the tribulation. They focus on the practices of the Jewish faith while under the Law of Moses. During the tribulation period the Jewish people will once again practice the laws as ascribed to Moses, specifically, worshipping and offering sacrifices in the re-built temple.

**Revelation 2:6**
*But this you have, that you hate the deeds of the Nicolaitans, which I also hate.*

**Revelation 2:9**
*I know your works, tribulation, and poverty (but you are rich); and I know the blasphemy of those who say they are Jews and are not, but are a synagogue of Satan.*

**Revelation 2:14**
*But I have a few things against you, because you have there those who hold the doctrine of Balaam, who taught Balak to put a stumbling block before the children of Israel, to eat things sacrificed to idols, and to commit sexual immorality.*

**Revelation 2:20**
*Nevertheless I have a few things against you, because you allow that woman Jezebel, who calls herself a prophetess, to teach and seduce My servants to commit sexual immorality and eat things sacrificed to idols.*

It is clear that the messages are directed to churches that existed in the past and were struggling during John's time and those who will be existing during the tribulation period. The message to those in the tribulation period is *he who overcomes* will receive His reward, namely the right to have everlasting life. *He who overcomes* ties in directly to Christ's words in Matthew.

**Matthew 24:13**
*But he who endures to the end shall be saved.*

Of interest, note the references to events that will involve the churches during the tribulation period:

**Revelation 2:10**
*Do not fear any of those things which you are about to suffer. Indeed, the devil is about to throw some of you into prison,*

*that you may be tested, and you will have tribulation ten days. Be faithful until death, and I will give you the crown of life.*

This event will occur after Satan has been cast to the earth, this subject is discussed in this book when the war in heaven takes place and the angel Michael, who stands for Israel, will cast Satan to the earth. Satan then will try to annihilate Israel during Jacob's time of trouble (the 75-day period at the end).

### Revelation 2:17

*"He who has an ear, let him hear what the Spirit says to the churches. To him who overcomes I will give some of the hidden manna to eat. And I will give him a white stone, and on the stone a new name written which no one knows except him who receives it."*

This event will occur after the battle at Armageddon, when Christ remains on the earth to establish His kingdom on earth starting with the millennium (1000 years of peace). Immediately after Armageddon and the devastation on the earth, God will feed the people who will enter the millennium with the hidden manna.

### Ezekiel 34:13

*And I will bring them out from the peoples and gather them from the countries, and will bring them to their own land; I will feed them on the mountains of Israel, in the valleys and in all the inhabited places of the country.*

### Revelation 2:26-28

*And he who overcomes, and keeps My works until the end, to him I will give power over the nations— ' He shall rule them with a rod of iron; They shall be dashed to pieces like the potter's vessels' — as I also have received from My Father; and I will give him the morning star.*

This event describes the right to those who overcome to rule the nations during the millennium with Christ.

### Revelation 3:12

*He who overcomes, I will make him a pillar in the temple of My God, and he shall go out no more. I will write on him the name of My God and the name of the city of My God, the New Jerusalem, which comes down out of heaven from My God. And I will write on him My new name.*

This event will occur for those who live in the millennium on the earth. The new Jerusalem will come from the new heaven to the new earth. Israel and adherents from the millennium will come to Mount Zion, to the city of the living God, and meet the angels, the church in heaven, and God and Jesus. They will enter God's kingdom at this time, transferred from the old earth to the new earth.

### See Also:

❑ *Hebrews 12:18-29.*

# Revelation Chapters 4, 5 & 6

After the messages to the churches, the first of the events that must take place, is a scene in heaven where God is on His throne and is holding in His right hand, a scroll that has been written on both sides and sealed with seven seals. This scroll is of great significance and a decision is made at the meeting in heaven that Christ is the only one worthy to break the seals of the scroll. Information about the contents of the scroll is given to us in Revelation 6, wherein we can determine the scroll contains God's control of His *judgment*s and wrath that He will be pouring out on the earth during the seven years plus 75 days of the tribulation period. The tribulation period is the time of the antichrist's kingdom during which God's Spirit will be active.

God Spirit is invisible and eternal.

### II Corinthians 4:18
*While we do not look at the things which are seen, but at the things which are not seen. For the things which are seen are temporary, but the things which are not seen are eternal.*

Because the spiritual world is invisible it is a mystery to man. Man can experience the Spirit more than he can understand it. Man certainly will experience both the spirit of light and the spirit of darkness in the world during the events of the proclaimed period of tribulation. God's spirit is not a single entity, but is a multiphase Spirit who controls everything He created. References to His Spirit are many, the following list are but a few:

- Seven Spirits of God are lamps of fire before His throne.

### Revelation 4:5
*….Seven lamps of fire were burning before the throne, which are the seven Spirits of God.*

- Christ the Lamb has seven horns and <u>seven eyes</u> which are the seven Spirits of God.

## Revelation 5:6
*And I looked, and behold, in the midst of the throne and of the four living creatures, and in the midst of the elders, stood a Lamb as though it had been slain, having seven horns and seven eyes, which are the seven Spirits of God sent out into all the earth.*

## Zechariah 4:10
*For who has despised the day of small things? For these seven rejoice to see the plumb line in the hand of Zerubbabel. They are the eyes of the LORD, which scan to and fro throughout the whole earth."*

- Four Spirits of heaven are described as four horses that go out into all the earth.

## Zechariah 1:7-11
*On the twenty-fourth day of the eleventh month, which is the month Shebat, in the second year of Darius, the word of the LORD came to Zechariah the son of Berechiah, the son of Iddo the prophet: I saw by night, and behold, a man riding on a red horse, and it stood among the myrtle trees in the hollow; and behind him were horses: red, sorrel, and white. Then I said, "My lord, what are these?" So the angel who talked with me said to me, "I will show you what they are." And the man who stood among the myrtle trees answered and said, "These are the ones whom the LORD has sent to walk to and fro throughout the earth." So they answered the Angel of the LORD, who stood among the myrtle trees, and said, "We have walked to and fro throughout the earth, and behold, all the earth is resting quietly."*

## Zechariah 6:5-8

*And the angel answered and said to me, "These are four spirits of heaven, who go out from their station before the Lord of all the earth. The one with the black horses is going to the north country, the white are going after them,*

*and the dappled are going toward the south country." Then the strong steeds went out, eager to go, that they might walk to and fro throughout the earth. And He said, "Go, walk to and fro throughout the earth." So they walked to and fro throughout the earth. And He called to me, and spoke to me, saying, "See, those who go toward the north country have given rest to My Spirit in the north country."*

- The white horse and Christ with the sword in His mouth are God's Spirit coming to Armageddon.

## Revelation 19:11

*Now I saw heaven opened, and behold, a white horse. And He who sat on him was called Faithful and True, and in righteousness He judges and makes war.*

- Having regard for God's words about horses being His Spirits, we can conclude the white horse, red horse, black horse, and pale horse which come with the breaking of the first four seals of the scroll, are God's Spirits allowing the antichrist to establish his kingdom and bringing the respective consequences of His judgments to the earth.

## First Seal

### Revelation 6:1

*Now I saw when the Lamb opened one of the seals; and I heard one of the four living creatures saying with a voice like thunder, "Come and see."*

When Christ opens the first seal the tribulation period begins, and it will last for seven years and 75 days. The antichrist makes his appearance as a king at war.

### Revelation 6:2

*And I looked, and behold, a white horse. He who sat on it had a bow; and a crown was given to him, and he went out conquering and to conquer.*

### Revelation 13:5

*And he was given a mouth speaking great things and blasphemies, and he was given authority to continue for forty-two months.*

The tribulation period has been divided into two periods of equal time and there will be a ruler for each period. The ruler during the first period is the beast who rises from the sea. This is the antichrist.

### Revelation 13:1

*Then I stood on the sand of the sea. And I saw a beast rising up out of the sea, having seven heads and ten horns, and on his horns ten crowns, and on his heads a blasphemous name.*

## Second, Third, and Fourth Seals

### Revelation 6: 3-8

*When He opened the second seal, I heard the second living creature saying, "Come and see." Another horse, fiery red, went out. And it was granted to the one who sat on it to take peace from the earth, and that people should kill one another; and there was given to him a great sword. When He opened the third seal, I heard the third living creature say, "Come and see." So I looked, and behold, a black horse, and he who sat on it had a pair of scales in his hand. And I heard a voice in the midst of the four living creatures saying, "A quart of wheat for a denarius, and three quarts of barley for a denarius; and do not harm the oil and the wine." When He opened the fourth seal, I heard the voice of the fourth living creature saying, "Come and see." So I looked, and behold, a pale horse. And the name of him who sat on it was Death, and Hades followed with him. And power was given to them over a fourth of the earth, to kill with sword, with hunger, with death, and by the beasts of the earth.*

With the opening of the second, third, and fourth seals we see that peace is taken from the earth and people are killing each other, a famine will occur and the rider of the pale horse was called Death and Hades.

## Fifth Seal

### Revelation 6:9-11

*When He opened the fifth seal, I saw under the altar the souls of those who had been slain for the word of God and for the testimony which they held. And they cried with a loud voice, saying, "How long, O Lord, holy and true, until You judge and avenge our blood on those who dwell on the earth?" Then a white robe was given to each of them; and it was said to them that they should rest a little while longer, until both the number of their fellow servants and their brethren, who would be killed as they were, was completed.*

The souls John saw under the altar were the martyrs taken to heaven after they had been slain for the word of God and their testimony. We know they were taken to heaven because they are under the altar, given white robes and told to rest a little longer. These martyrs under the altar will join the resurrection of the great multitude according to Revelation 7.

### See Also:

❑ *Chapter 1: God versus Satan - the Period of Grace.*
❑ *Chapter 10: Revelation - Revelation Chapter 7*

## Sixth Seal

### Revelation 6:12-16
*I looked when He opened the sixth seal, and behold, there was a great earthquake; and the sun became black as sackcloth of hair, and the moon became like blood. And the stars of heaven fell to the earth, as a fig tree drops its late figs when it is shaken by a mighty wind. Then the sky receded as a scroll when it is rolled up, and every mountain and island was moved out of its place. And the kings of the earth, the great men, the rich men, the commanders, the mighty men, every slave and every free man, hid themselves in the caves and in the rocks of the mountains, and said to the mountains and rocks, "Fall on us and hide us from the face of Him who sits on the throne and from the wrath of the Lamb!*

This earth shaking and cosmic catastrophe occurs at the beginning of the second half of the tribulation, when God's day of wrath comes upon the earth as foretold in Zephaniah.

### Zephaniah 1:16-17
*A day of trumpet and alarm against the fortified cities and against the high towers. "I will bring distress upon men, And they shall walk like blind men, Because they have sinned against the Lord; Their blood shall be poured out like dust, And their flesh like refuse."*

# Revelation Chapter 7

## Sealing of the 144,000

Starting in Revelation Chapter 7 we read about the sealing of the 144,000 Israelites who are called the servants of our God. All of the 12 tribes are listed and we are told that 12,000 of each tribe receive the seal of God on their foreheads. These seals will provide God's protection for the Israelites, who are called His servants, from the wrath that God will pour out in the second half of the tribulation period. After the sealing there is the resurrection of a great multitude of all nations, tribes and people standing before the Lamb in heaven. In the pursuing discussion between John and one of the elders in this vision, John is informed by the elder that these are the people who have come through the great tribulation and have washed their robes and made them white in the blood of the Lamb. For this reason they become servants of God in heaven and will serve God throughout eternity. The resurrection of this great multitude happens at mid-tribulation. The martyrs under the altar are told to rest a little while longer until their fellow servants and brethren will be killed as they were. These are the martyrs who will join the resurrection of the great multitude.

# Revelation Chapter 8

## Seventh Seal

God commissions the seven angels who stood before Him to sound their trumpets and bring revenge on the earth, this begins the second half of the tribulation wherein God's wrath is about to start. The events of the trumpets are as follows:

### 1ˢᵗ Trumpet:

Hail, fire, and blood thrown to the earth; one third of the trees and grass will be burned.

### Revelation 8:7
*The first angel sounded: And hail and fire followed, mingled with blood, and they were thrown to the earth. And a third of the trees were burned up, and all green grass was burned up.*

### 2ⁿᵈ Trumpet:

A mountain of fire is thrown into the sea and one third of the sea becomes blood. One third of the living creatures in the sea will die.

### Revelation 8:8-9
*Then the second angel sounded: And something like a great mountain burning with fire was thrown into the sea, and a third of the sea became blood. And a third of the living creatures in the sea died, and a third of the ships were destroyed.*

### 3ʳᵈ Trumpet:

A star falls from heaven on one third of the rivers and on the springs of water, and the waters become wormwood and men will die from the bitter water.

## Revelation 8:10-11

*Then the third angel sounded: And a great star fell from heaven, burning like a torch, and it fell on a third of the rivers and on the springs of water. The name of the star is Wormwood. A third of the waters became wormwood, and many men died from the water, because it was made bitter.*

## 4th Trumpet:

One third of the sun, moon and stars are struck and this adversely affects the light, both day and night.

## Revelation 8:12

*Then the fourth angel sounded: And a third of the sun was struck, a third of the moon, and a third of the stars, so that a third of them were darkened. A third of the day did not shine, and likewise the night.*

## Revelation 8:13

*And I looked, and I heard an angel flying through the midst of heaven, saying with a loud voice, "Woe, woe, woe to the inhabitants of the earth, because of the remaining blasts of the trumpet of the three angels who are about to sound!"*

# Revelation Chapter 9

**5ᵗʰ Trumpet:**

Locusts come from the bottomless pit. These locusts will sting men like scorpions, and due to the pain men will seek death but will not find it. The locusts are directed not to eat grass, but to hurt men for 5 months.

**Revelation 9:1-12**

*Then the fifth angel sounded: And I saw a star fallen from heaven to the earth. To him was given the key to the bottomless pit. And he opened the bottomless pit, and smoke arose out of the pit like the smoke of a great furnace. So the sun and the air were darkened because of the smoke of the pit. Then out of the smoke locusts came upon the earth. And to them was given power, as the scorpions of the earth have power. They were commanded not to harm the grass of the earth, or any green thing, or any tree, but only those men who do not have the seal of God on their foreheads. And they were not given authority to kill them, but to torment them for five months. Their torment was like the torment of a scorpion when it strikes a man. In those days men will seek death and will not find it; they will desire to die, and death will flee from them. The shape of the locusts was like horses prepared for battle. On their heads were crowns of something like gold, and their faces were like the faces of men. They had hair like women's hair, and their teeth were like lions' teeth. And they had breastplates like breastplates of iron, and the sound of their wings was like the sound of chariots with many horses running into battle. They had tails like scorpions, and there were stings in their tails. Their power was to hurt men five months. And they had as king over them the angel of the bottomless pit, whose name in Hebrew is Abaddon, but in*

*Greek he has the name Apollyon. One woe is past. Behold, still two more woes are coming after these things.*

## 6th Trumpet:

Four angels come out of the Euphrates river and they command an army of two hundred million who will kill one third of mankind with fire, smoke, and brimstone which comes out of the mouths of the horses they are riding. The rest of mankind who were not killed by this plague, do not repent but continue in all their sins.

## Revelation 9:13-21

*Then the sixth angel sounded: And I heard a voice from the four horns of the golden altar which is before God, saying to the sixth angel who had the trumpet, "Release the four angels who are bound at the great river Euphrates." So the four angels, who had been prepared for the hour and day and month and year, were released to kill a third of mankind. Now the number of the army of the horsemen was two hundred million; I heard the number of them. And thus I saw the horses in the vision: those who sat on them had breastplates of fiery red, hyacinth blue, and sulfur yellow; and the heads of the horses were like the heads of lions; and out of their mouths came fire, smoke, and brimstone. By these three plagues a third of mankind was killed—by the fire and the smoke and the brimstone which came out of their mouths. For their power is in their mouth and in their tails; for their tails are like serpents, having heads; and with them they do harm. But the rest of mankind, who were not killed by these plagues, did not repent of the works of their hands, that they should not worship demons, and idols of gold, silver, brass, stone, and wood, which can neither see nor hear nor walk. And they did not repent of their murders or their sorceries or their sexual immorality or their thefts.*

# Revelation Chapters 10 & 11

John had a vision of mid-tribulation, wherein a mighty angel from heaven has a little book open in his hand. This angel sets his right foot on the sea and his left foot on the land and cries out with a loud voice and seven thunders utter their voices. John was instructed not to write what the thunders utter. God told John to take the little book and eat it. The book was sweet as honey in his mouth but made his stomach bitter. Then John was told to prophesy again.

### Revelation 10:11
*And he said to me, "You must prophesy again about many peoples, nations, tongues, and kings."*

John's whole life was involved in the ministry. He wrote the books of John, I, II, and III John, and Revelation. He was no stranger to the gospel or prophecy and was told that he must prophesy again to the whole world.

When would this occur? Following the chronological sequence in the vision, he eats the book, measures the temple of the tribulation period and is informed by Christ that He will provide power to two witnesses to prophesy for 1260 days in sack cloth. The account of the ministry of the two witnesses is given in Revelation 11.

### Revelation 11: 4-13
*These are the two olive trees and the two lampstands standing before the God of the earth. And if anyone wants to harm them, fire proceeds from their mouth and devours their enemies. And if anyone wants to harm them, he must be killed in this manner. These have power to shut heaven, so that no rain falls in the days of their prophecy; and they have power over waters to turn them to blood, and to strike the earth with all plagues, as often as they desire. When they finish their testimony, the beast that ascends out of the bottomless*

*pit will make war against them, overcome them, and kill them. And their dead bodies will lie in the street of the great city which spiritually is called Sodom and Egypt, where also our Lord was crucified. Then those from the peoples, tribes, tongues, and nations will see their dead bodies three-and-a-half days, and not allow their dead bodies to be put into graves. And those who dwell on the earth will rejoice over them, make merry, and send gifts to one another, because these two prophets tormented those who dwell on the earth. Now after the three-and-a-half days the breath of life from God entered them, and they stood on their feet, and great fear fell on those who saw them. And they heard a loud voice from heaven saying to them, "Come up here." And they ascended to heaven in a cloud, and their enemies saw them. In the same hour there was a great earthquake, and a tenth of the city fell. In the earthquake seven thousand people were killed, and the rest were afraid and gave glory to the God of heaven.*

In Revelation Chapter 10, John is given the distinct command that he will have to prophesy again in the tribulation period, making him one of the two witnesses. We know from Malachi, that Elijah will be the other witness.

### Revelation 10:10-11
*Then I took the little book out of the angel's hand and ate it, and it was as sweet as honey in my mouth. But when I had eaten it, my stomach became bitter. And he said to me, "You must prophesy again about many peoples, nations, tongues, and kings."*

### Malachi 4:5,6
*Behold, I will send you Elijah the prophet before the coming of the great and dreadful day of the Lord. And he will turn the hearts of the fathers to the children, and the hearts of the children to their fathers, lest I come and strike the earth with a curse.*

**7<sup>th</sup> Trumpet:**

At the sounding of the seventh trumpet, the mystery of God will be finished and Christ's millennium kingdom will be established. Note in Revelation 10:7 ***"but in the days of the sounding of the seventh angel",*** the expression of days allows time for the 75-day period after the 1260 days of the second half of the tribulation. There is also mention of God's wrath, ***judgment*** and rewards to the prophets and servants at this trumpet sounding. Chronologically, this ***judgment*** ties into the ***judgment*** spoken of in Revelation 11:15-18, and the time when the two witnesses are also resurrected.

**Revelation 11:15-18**
*Then the seventh angel sounded: And there were loud voices in heaven, saying, "The kingdoms of this world have become the kingdoms of our Lord and of His Christ, and He shall reign forever and ever!" And the twenty-four elders who sat before God on their thrones fell on their faces and worshiped God, saying: "We give You thanks, O Lord God Almighty, The One who is and who was and who is to come, because You have taken Your great power and reigned. The nations were angry, and Your wrath has come, and the time of the dead, that they should be judged, and that You should reward Your servants the prophets and the saints, and those who fear Your name, small and great, and should destroy those who destroy the earth.*

# Revelation Chapter 12

John first has a vision of a woman, who is the nation of Israel. He then sees the fiery red dragon with 7 heads and 10 horns and seven diadems on his head that is Satan. One third of the angels in heaven go with Satan and he goes to devour the woman as soon as her child was born, and the child is taken to God. Then the woman enters the second half of the tribulation. The next event is the war in heaven, when Michael fights with Satan and Satan is cast to the earth. When the dragon is cast to the earth he persecutes the woman.

### Revelation 12:14
*But the woman was given two wings of a great eagle, that she might fly into the wilderness to her place, where she is nourished for a time and times and half a time, from the presence of the serpent.*

The presence of the serpent results from the war in heaven when Satan was cast to the earth. The two wings of an eagle represents God's help to allow Israel to flee into the wilderness.

### Revelation 12:7-9
*And war broke out in heaven: Michael and his angels fought with the dragon; and the dragon and his angels fought, but they did not prevail, nor was a place found for them in heaven any longer. So the great dragon was cast out, that serpent of old, called the Devil and Satan, who deceives the whole world; he was cast to the earth, and his angels were cast out with him.*

### Revelation 12:13
*Now when the dragon saw that he had been cast to the earth, he persecuted the woman who gave birth to the male Child.*

## Revelation 12:1-2

*...a women clothed with the sun, with the moon under her feet, and on her head a garland of twelve stars. Then being with child she cried out in labour and in pain to give birth.*

The woman as described in this verse, is the nation of Israel.

## Revelation 17: 1-2

*...the great harlot who sits on many waters, with whom the kings of the earth committed fornication, and the inhabitants of the earth were made drunk with the wine of her fornication.*

The great harlot in this passage is the antichrist's kingdom under Satan's control who will attempt to annihilate Israel. God will intervene and protect Israel (the woman) who will flee into the wilderness that God has prepared, and He will care for *her* for 1260 days.

Chronologically this brings Israel to the last half of the tribulation period (1260 days or 3 ½ years). The scene then changes to the war in heaven wherein Satan and his fallen angels are cast to the earth and Israel is confronted with the worst time of trouble the world has ever seen, namely Jacob's time of trouble (time, times and half of a time). This is the 75-day period that was described in Daniel Chapter 12. During Jacob's time of trouble Satan will attempt to annihilate Israel but God provides His help (*wings of an eagle*), to carry Israel into the wilderness and to nourish her there until Christ comes from heaven to fight the battle at Armageddon. This whole scene is described in Revelation 12:13-17.

# Revelation Chapter 13

John had a vision of a beast from the sea who had seven heads and ten horns. The beast he saw was like a leopard with the feet of a bear and a mouth of a lion. In Daniel's vision the lion was Babylon (Daniel7:4), the bear was Media-Persia (Daniel 7:5), and the leopard with four heads was Greece (Daniel 7:6). The fourth beast was distinct from the others and had 10 horns. This kingdom with iron teeth was Rome (Daniel 7:7), and will eventually develop into the kingdom of the antichrist in the latter days.

**Daniel 7: 4-7**

*The first was like a lion, and had eagle's wings. I watched till its wings were plucked off; and it was lifted up from the earth and made to stand on two feet like a man, and a man's heart was given to it. And suddenly another beast, a second, like a bear. It was raised up on one side, and had three ribs in its mouth between its teeth. And they said thus to it: 'Arise, devour much flesh!' After this I looked, and there was another, like a leopard, which had on its back four wings of a bird. The beast also had four heads, and dominion was given to it. After this I saw in the night visions, and behold, a fourth beast, dreadful and terrible, exceedingly strong. It had huge iron teeth; it was devouring, breaking in pieces, and trampling the residue with its feet. It was different from all the beasts that were before it, and it had ten horns.*

The kingdoms Daniel saw during his time are now historical. Daniel was informed that his visions of these kingdoms would be part of the events of the latter days.

### Daniel 8:17
*So he came near where I stood, and when he came I was afraid and fell on my face; but he said to me, "Understand, son of man, that the vision refers to the time of the end."*

We know Babylon today is called Iraq, Media-Persia is now Iran, Greece is still Greece, and Rome was headquartered in Italy. This kingdom was and still is diverse in that it would spread into and devour the whole earth. The Roman empire historically covered much of Europe and we are still in the aftermath of this kingdom today; the *"one is"* kingdom is now worldwide. The seventh kingdom of John's vision is still to come in the future. It is the beast with seven heads and ten horns which will constitute the antichrist's kingdom. The seven heads are going to be present day countries who will be united under a covenant.

### Daniel 9:27
*Then he shall confirm a covenant with many for one week; but in the middle of the week He shall bring an end to sacrifice and offering. And on the wing of abominations shall be one who makes desolate, even until the consummation, which is determined, is poured out on the desolate.*

In Revelation 13, the description of the beast, namely, leopard, bear, and lion, suggest that the historical kingdoms will also be the present day countries with names different from the historical ones, and these will become the kingdom of the antichrist. This kingdom will have a king.

### Revelation 6:2
*And I looked, and behold, a white horse. He who sat on it had a bow; and a crown was given to him, and he went out conquering and to conquer.*

This king will be empowered by the dragon.

**Revelation 13:2**

*Now the beast which I saw was like a leopard, his feet were like the feet of a bear, and his mouth like the mouth of a lion. The dragon gave him his power, his throne, and great authority.*

He has a blasphemous mouth and will have authority to continue for 42 months. He will make war with Israel, and all non-believers will worship him. He will control the whole world.

**Revelation 13:7**

*It was granted to him to make war with the saints and to overcome them. And authority was given him over every tribe, tongue, and nation.*

One of his heads is wounded and healed.

**Revelation 13:3**

*And I saw one of his heads as if it had been mortally wounded, and his deadly wound was healed. And all the world marvelled and followed the beast.*

**Revelation 17:9-10**

*Here is the mind which has wisdom: The seven heads are seven mountains on which the woman sits. There are also seven kings. Five have fallen, one is, and the other has not yet come. And when he comes, he must continue a short time.*

**Revelation 17:15**

*Then he said to me, "The waters which you saw, where the harlot sits, are peoples, multitudes, nations, and tongues.*

The mountains are different countries or kingdoms with representative kings. The waters in Revelation 17:15 are peoples, multitudes, nations, and tongues. The nations mentioned are giving their support to the beast, which is the antichrist's kingdom. The antichrist is talked about in Revelation 17:10, when it says *"when he comes, he must continue a short time."* A short time is the 42 months.

Then in Revelation 17:11 we read about the false prophet.

### Revelation 17:11

*And the beast that was, and is not, is himself also the eighth, and is of the seven, and is going to perdition.*

In Revelation 13:11 John has the vision of another beast coming up out of the earth, and the beast had two horns like a lamb and spoke like a dragon.

This is the false prophet who wants to have people think he is Christ, but he is empowered by Satan because he speaks like a dragon. Through the evil power of Satan he will perform great signs and do magical things like making fire come down from heaven. He is very deceptive and builds an image in honor of the antichrist, and he gives breath to this image so the image can speak. The false prophet will have killed, anyone who refuses to worship the image. He will attempt to enforce everyone to receive a mark in their right hand or forehead.

### Revelation 13:11-18

*Then I saw another beast coming up out of the earth, and he had two horns like a lamb and spoke like a dragon. And he exercises all the authority of the first beast in his presence, and causes the earth and those who dwell in it to worship the first beast, whose deadly wound was healed. He performs great signs, so that he even makes fire come down from heaven on the earth in the sight of men. And he deceives those who dwell on the earth by those signs which he was granted to do in the sight of the beast, telling those who dwell on the earth to make an image to the beast who was wounded by the sword and lived. He was granted power to give breath to the image of the beast, that the image of the beast should both speak and cause as many as would not worship the image of the beast to be killed. He causes all, both small and great, rich and poor, free and slave, to receive a mark on their right hand or on their foreheads, and that no one may buy or sell except one who has the mark or the name of the beast, or the number of his name. Here is wisdom. Let him who has understanding calculate the number of the beast, for it is the number of a man: His number is 666.*

# Revelation Chapter 14

John sees the 144,000 who were sealed at mid-tribulation, standing with Christ on Mount Zion. These are redeemed from among men and will be the first to enter the millennial kingdom because they are referred to as the first fruits to God and to the Lamb. The vision then shifts to the angel who will preach the everlasting gospel to those on earth, to every nation, tribe, tongue, and people. After this he talks about the judgment of Babylon and then to the warning for people not to take the mark of the beast or they would be tormented in the lake of fire forever.

**Revelation 14:1-5**
*Then I looked, and behold, a Lamb standing on Mount Zion, and with Him one hundred and forty-four thousand, having His Father's name written on their foreheads. And I heard a voice from heaven, like the voice of many waters, and like the voice of loud thunder. And I heard the sound of harpists playing their harps. They sang as it were a new song before the throne, before the four living creatures, and the elders; and no one could learn that song except the hundred and forty-four thousand who were redeemed from the earth. These are the ones who were not defiled with women, for they are virgins. These are the ones who follow the Lamb wherever He goes. These were redeemed from among men, being firstfruits to God and to the Lamb. And in their mouth was found no deceit, for they are without fault before the throne of God.*

## The 144,000

This group has been selected by God to receive full protection. 144,000 are sealed and Christ takes 144,000 into heaven where they are taught a new song by the harpists around the throne. We determine this group is a group of men, as they were not defiled by women but are virgins, they did not lie, and they are without fault before God.

### Isaiah 61:6
*But you shall be named the priests of the Lord, they shall call you the servants of our God.*

The 144,000 will follow the Lamb (Christ) into the millennium kingdom. They do not enter heaven ahead of the believing Jews who went by the pre-tribulation rapture, nor those who were resurrected at mid-tribulation and went to heaven. To be first fruits, therefore, they are scheduled to go into the millennial kingdom of Christ on the earth, where they will be first fruits and where they will be singers or priests in the millennial temple that is to be built for the millennial period. The high standards of their lives suggest a form of priesthood fit for service to God. Since they were taught a song they likely are singers. They will be singers in the millennial temple.

### Ezekiel 40:44-45
*Outside the inner gate were the chambers for the singers in the inner court, one facing south at the side of the northern gateway. Then he said to me, "This chamber which faces south is for the priests who have charge of the temple.*

Thus it appears that God specifically chose the 144,000 because He had a purpose for them in the future.

## Judgment of Babylon

The judgment of Babylon is God's judgment of the world's nations, their trading systems and living conditions. This judgment involves plagues, death, and mourning. It will be short, it will come in one day and God will destroy the entire system and way of life. Additional details of this judgment are given in Revelation 16:17-21

## Mark of the Beast

This end-time event is a man-made scheme (under the control of Satan) that is the greatest of all abominations to God, because man is forced to worship Satan. God issues a special warning to people, not to take the mark of the beast.

### Revelation 14:9-11

*Then a third angel followed them, saying with a loud voice, "If anyone worships the beast and his image, and receives his mark on his forehead or on his hand, he himself shall also drink of the wine of the wrath of God, which is poured out full strength into the cup of His indignation. He shall be tormented with fire and brimstone in the presence of the holy angels and in the presence of the Lamb. And the smoke of their torment ascends forever and ever; and they have no rest day or night, who worship the beast and his image, and whoever receives the mark of his name."*

The originator of the scheme is the false prophet.

### Revelation 13: 14-18

*And he deceives those who dwell on the earth by those signs which he was granted to do in the sight of the beast, telling those who dwell on the earth to make an image to the beast who was wounded by the sword and lived. He was granted power to give breath to the image of the beast, that the image of the beast should both speak and cause as many as would not worship the image of the beast to be killed. He causes all, both small and great, rich and poor, free and slave, to receive a mark on their right hand or on their foreheads, and that no one may buy or sell except one who has the mark or[b] the name of the beast, or the number of his name. Here is wisdom. Let him who has understanding calculate the number of the beast, for it is the number of a man: His number is 666.*

This end-time scheme has similar characteristics of the one Antiochus Epiphanes undertook; when he placed the statue of the god Jupiter Olympius on the altar in the temple to establish Greek worship, and then proceeded to kill all those who did not conform.

### Daniel 8:23

*And in the latter time of their kingdom, when the transgressors have reached their fullness, a king shall arise, having fierce features, who understands sinister schemes.*

The basics of the end-time scheme are similar, starting with an image of the beast, enforcing worship of the image and the beast, with the worship being controlled by the mark or number, and the killing of all who do not conform.

## Last Harvest (Sickle)

Harvest is a time when the planter reaps what is his, and the last harvest is the time that Christ will take the last souls of men that He will reap prior to the battle at Armageddon.

### Revelation 14:14-16

*Then I looked, and behold, a white cloud, and on the cloud sat One like the Son of Man, having on His head a golden crown, and in His hand a sharp sickle. And another angel came out of the temple, crying with a loud voice to Him who sat on the cloud, "Thrust in Your sickle and reap, for the time has come for You to reap, for the harvest of the earth is ripe." So He who sat on the cloud thrust in His sickle on the earth, and the earth was reaped.*

Note that this is a harvest. In this reaping Christ takes the people who were victorious over the beast, who did not take his mark. Contrast this with the sickle the next angel will use.

**Armageddon (Sickle)**

**Revelation 14:17-20**

*Then another angel came out of the temple which is in heaven, he also having a sharp sickle. And another angel came out from the altar, who had power over fire, and he cried with a loud cry to him who had the sharp sickle, saying, "Thrust in your sharp sickle and gather the clusters of the vine of the earth, for her grapes are fully ripe." So the angel thrust his sickle into the earth and gathered the vine of the earth, and threw it into the great winepress of the wrath of God. And the winepress was trampled outside the city, and blood came out of the winepress, up to the horses' bridles, for one thousand six hundred furlongs.*

This clearly describes a war, not a harvest and it is the description of the battle at Armageddon.

# Revelation Chapter 15

The vision begins with a view of the angels with the seven last plagues that complete God's wrath. John then sees the people who were victorious over the beast, the mark of the beast or the number of his name, standing on something like a sea of glass mingled with fire, and they were singing the song of Moses and the Lamb. This means they were taken into heaven where they will wait until they will be taken into the millennium.

**Revelation 4:6**
*Before the throne there was[a] a sea of glass, like crystal.*

**Revelation 20:4**
*And I saw thrones, and they sat on them, and judgment was committed to them. Then I saw the souls of those who had been beheaded for their witness to Jesus and for the word of God, who had not worshiped the beast or his image, and had not received his mark on their foreheads or on their hands. And they lived and reigned with Christ for a thousand years.*

The next part of the vision shows the preparation in heaven of the seven angels who will pour out the seven bowls of wrath onto the earth.

# Revelation Chapter 16

The seven last plagues that complete the wrath of God are the bowl judgments. There are seven angels appointed to pour out the bowls of wrath.

### 1st Bowl - Loathsome Sores

Foul and loathsome sores come upon those who have the mark of the beast.

### 2nd Bowl - The Sea Turns to Blood

This bowl is poured on the sea and every living creature in the sea dies.

### 3rd Bowl - The Waters Turn to Blood

Rivers and springs of water are turned to blood; avengement for the blood of the saints and prophets.

### 4th Bowl - Men Are Scorched

Men will be scorched by the sun with fire.

### 5th Bowl - Darkness and Pain

God judges the beast's kingdom which became full of darkness and men will be in great pain.

### 6th Bowl - Euphrates Dried Up

The Euphrates river is dried up so the way for the kings of the east will be prepared. The spirits of demons will perform signs to the kings of the earth to gather them for Armageddon. Note the dragon, beast, and false prophet are working together in the antichrist's kingdom.

### 7th Bowl - The Earth Utterly Shaken

God says "*it is done*" and the biggest earth-quake the earth has ever seen will occur. The cities of the nations will fall, every island will disappear and all the mountains will not be found. Great hail will fall. This is actu-ally the *judgment* of Babylon the Great, that great world system referred to as *a city*. This is fully described in Revelation Chapter 18.

### Revelation 16:12-14

*Then the sixth angel poured out his bowl on the great river Euphrates, and its water was dried up, so that the way of the kings from the east might be prepared. And I saw three unclean spirits like frogs coming out of the mouth of the dragon, out of the mouth of the beast, and out of the mouth of the false prophet. For they are spirits of demons, performing signs, which go out to the kings of the earth and of the whole world, to gather them to the battle of that great day of God Almighty.*

The dragon, beast, and false prophet are all deceiving the nations with the power of evil spirits, performing signs to gather them for the battle at Armageddon. This ties into the earlier comments that all three work together in the antichrist's kingdom.

### Judgment of Babylon

### Revelation 16:17-21

*Then the seventh angel poured out his bowl into the air, and a loud voice came out of the temple of heaven, from the throne, saying, "It is done!" And there were noises and thun-derings and lightnings; and there was a great earthquake, such a mighty and great earthquake as had not occurred since men were on the earth. Now the great city was divided into three parts, and the cities of the nations fell. And great Babylon was remembered before God, to give her the cup of the wine of the fierceness of His wrath. Then every island fled away, and the mountains were not found. And great hail from heaven fell upon men, each hailstone about the weight of a talent. Men blasphemed God because of the plague of the hail, since that plague was exceedingly great.*

The judgment starts with the biggest earthquake ever to occur on the earth. The great city was divided into 3 parts, all the cities of the nations fell. Every island and mountain will be removed and there will be great hail, with hailstones the weight of a talon (more than 100 lbs).

# Revelation Chapter 17

Satan's principalities and powers of darkness were exercised in the beginning, the Garden of Eden, and ever since have continued throughout history. In the next kingdom to come he will be the power base. The seven heads of Satan's kingdom will be seven nations with a representative ruler or king.

**Revelation 12:3**

*And another sign appeared in heaven: behold, a great, fiery red dragon having seven heads and ten horns, and seven diadems on his heads.*

The satanic system of ruling kingdoms described in Revelation Chapter 17, is referred to as *the harlot*, starting with the kingdom of Babylon and climaxing with seven of the nations under a covenant called the seven heads. These nations will be ruled by the antichrist in the future, the next kingdom to control the earth. We know that it started with the historical kingdom of Babylon.

**Revelation 17:5**

*And on her forehead a name was written: Mystery, Babylon The Great, The Mother Of Harlots And Of The Abominations Of The Earth.*

**Revelation 17:1, 2**

*Then one of the seven angels who had the seven bowls came and talked with me, saying to me, "Come, I will show you the judgment of the great harlot who sits on many waters, with whom the kings of the earth committed fornication, and the inhabitants of the earth were made drunk with the wine of her fornication."*

Satan is the spirit of the antichrist, and our society today is becoming more anti-Christ in spirit as time moves on. God is being ridiculed more and more and His word will soon be forbidden everywhere and eventually in the next kingdom they will be worshipers of Satan rather than God.

### Revelation 13:4

*So they worshiped the dragon who gave authority to the beast; and they worshiped the beast, saying, "Who is like the beast? Who is able to make war with him?"*

The seven heads are seven nations under a covenant, which the antichrist will make. The seven heads compose *the harlot*, being the beginning and prime foundation of the antichrist's kingdom and its main power base. After a period of about three and one half years, the harlot will have the addition of the ten horns.

### Revelation 17:12,13

*"The ten horns which you saw are ten kings who have received no kingdom as yet, but they receive authority for one hour as kings with the beast. These are of one mind, and they will give their power and authority to the beast.*

To summarize the above discussion, we have established the following:

- Satan will empower two antichrist rulers; namely, the first beast - the antichrist, and the false prophet, who will each rule the kingdom for a three and one half year period, or a total of seven years. Satan carries the kingdom.

### Revelation 17:3

*So he carried me away in the Spirit into the wilderness. And I saw a woman sitting on a scarlet beast which was full of names of blasphemy, having seven heads and ten horns.*

- The first beast (antichrist) will start the kingdom with seven heads; being seven nations under a covenant. Then in the *last hour* of his three and one half year period, he will authorize ten kings (ten horns) to rule. This now becomes the kingdom of seven heads and ten horns.
- At mid-tribulation (the middle of the seven year period) the false prophet takes over the kingdom, and in so doing he uproots three of the kings.

### Revelation 17:8
*The beast that you saw was, and is not, and will ascend out of the bottomless pit and go to perdition. And those who dwell on the earth will marvel, whose names are not written in the Book of Life from the foundation of the world, when they see the beast that was, and is not, and yet is.*

The ten horns and seven heads, along with many other nations, will make war with the Lamb at the battle at Armageddon:

### Revelation 17:14
*These will make war with the Lamb, and the Lamb will overcome them, for He is Lord of lords and King of kings; and those who are with Him are called, chosen, and faithful.*

The vision in chapter 17 starts with the judgment of the great harlot who sits on many waters. This is what we know about the antichrist and the false prophet and their respective kingdoms:

The woman has a name on her forehead – Mystery, Babylon The Great, The Mother of Harlots and The Abominations of the Earth.

The word mystery tells us that the interpretation of the meaning will be difficult to grasp. The angel told John that he would tell him the mystery of both the woman and the beast that carries her. The woman and the beast are integral parts of the antichrist's kingdom which will be the next kingdom in the world and it will control the whole world. In simplified terms the woman constitutes the components of the kingdom and the beast she rides is both the individual who heads up the kingdom and the kingdom itself.

The word *beast* is spoken of as an individual and as a kingdom, and one must decipher which one it is. There are two individuals, namely the antichrist and the false prophet, who will be rulers of the same kingdom. Furthermore, Satan and his fallen angels will be yet another component of this coming kingdom. Satan will empower both antichrist individuals and will be the spiritual power for the antichrist's kingdom. After Satan is thrown to the earth, he himself, will be persecuting Israel during time, times, and a half a time.

### Revelation 12:13
*Now when the dragon saw that he had been cast to the earth, he persecuted the woman who gave birth to the male Child.*

The ten horns that were seen by Daniel and John will be ten smaller kingdoms in the immediate mid-east area surrounding Israel. They come into power one hour (*literally 1 hour*) with the first beast and they will give their power and authority to the beast. The horns will hate the harlot and will lead the harlot into destruction. It is interesting that the harlot and the ten horns (actually 8 horns after the stout horn uproots three), are separate entities. This supports the words of Daniel 2:41, 42.

### Daniel 2:41,42
*Whereas you saw the feet and toes, partly of potter's clay and partly of iron, the kingdom shall be divided; yet the strength of the iron shall be in it, just as you saw the iron mixed with ceramic clay. And as the toes of the feet were partly of iron and partly of clay, so the kingdom shall be partly strong and partly fragile.*

The third entity which causes the kingdom to be partly weak is the presence of Satan's angels that do not mix with men.

### Daniel 2:43
*As you saw iron mixed with ceramic clay, they will mingle with the seed of men; but they will not adhere to one another, just as iron does not mix with clay.*

The subject matter of the antichrist's kingdom is easier to understand when we look at the words of Daniel and John and categorically summarize the information as follows:

## The Antichrist

| 1. | The king that appears after the first seal is broken. | Revelation 6:1 |
|---|---|---|
| 2. | The king that makes a covenant with many. | Daniel 9:27 |
| 3. | He will be empowered by Satan. | Revelation 13:2 |
| 4. | He magnifies himself and blasphemes God. | Daniel 11:36 |
| 5. | He is the king of the north. | Daniel 11:40 |
| 6. | He shall honour a strange God. | Daniel 11:39 |
| 7. | He shall divide the land for gain (establish 10 horns). | Daniel 11:39 |
| 8. | He will reign for 42 months. | Revelation 13:5 |
| 9. | He will headquarter between the seas and the holy mountain. | Daniel 11:35 |
| 10. | He will be a Greek citizen (leopard) | Revelation 13:2 |

## The Antichrist's Kingdom

| 1. | The kingdom is the beast out of the sea, having seven heads and ten horns. | Revelation 13:1-10 |
|---|---|---|
| 2. | The seven heads are united under a covenant with many. | Daniel 9:27 |

| 3. | The seven heads are the countries of the great harlot, described as seven mountains on which she sits (seven areas), they are peoples, multitudes and nations, and tongues. The great harlot consists of more than one country (covenant with many). | Revelation 17:1 Revelation 17:9 Revelation 17:55 |
|---|---|---|
| 4. | There will be seven kings of which five have fallen; they are, therefore, historical. One is and the other has not yet come, and the false prophet who is the beast that was, and is not will be the eighth and is of the seven. The "one is" kingdom was the kingdom of John's time and continues through our church age to the antichrist who has not yet come. | Revelation 17:10-12 |
| 5. | I believe the fallen historical kingdoms are Babylon, Media-Persia, Greece, Syria, and Rome. Babylon (Iraq), Media-Persia (Iran), and Greece are the lion, bear, and leopard of Daniel's vision and will be three of the heads in the antichrist's kingdom. Rome was headquartered in Italy during the Roman empire, but the aftermath of this kingdom is now worldwide. | Daniel 7:1-4 Revelation 13:2 |
| 6. | Syria will be a head, because this was the kingdom of Antiochus Epiphanes, who set up the abomination of desolation. | Daniel 8:11 |

| 7. | Italy will be a head because this is the Roman kingdom from which the iron and clay feet and toes come from. | Daniel 2:43 |
|---|---|---|
| 8. | The sixth head will arise from the "*one is*" worldwide kingdom but there is no information given as to who it might be. This will be a country in the mideast, possibly Turkey, in which the seven churches existed and also Pergamos is where Satan's headquarters will be after he is thrown to the earth. | Revelation 2:13 |
| 9. | The ten horns are ten kings who will receive authority for one hour as kings with the beast. They will make war with the Lamb; this will be the battle at Armageddon. They will be kings in the false prophet's reign, and give their authority to him. The beginning of the ten horns is in the latter part of the first antichrist's kingdom. They reign with him for one hour and then rule with the eighth head, the false prophet, until they go to the battle at Armageddon. All the hype about the ten horns being the **prominent** empire of the last days does not represent the truth. They are only a subordinate part of the last kingdom. | Revelation 17:12 |

## The False Prophet

The false prophet is the beast coming out of the earth.

### Revelation 13:11

*Then I saw another beast coming up out of the earth, and he had two horns like a lamb and spoke like a dragon.*

> **POINT OF INTEREST**
> Ten Horns Being European Nations
> The interpretation once given of the ten horns as the nations of the original European Common Market, has not been representative of the truth. The ten horns will come from the descendents of Esau, and in Daniel are referred to as the King of the South.
> *Revelation 17:13-14: "These are of one mind, and they will give their power and authority to the beast. These will make war with the Lamb, and the Lamb will overcome them, for He is Lord of lords and King of kings; and those who are with Him are called, chosen, and faithful."*

He is trying to deceive the world into thinking he is like Christ (*two horns like a lamb*). He comes on the scene at mid-tribulation and continues for 42 months. He honours the first beast with an image and makes people receive the mark of the beast.

### Revelation 13: 12-18

*And he exercises all the authority of the first beast in his presence, and causes the earth and those who dwell in it to worship the first beast, whose deadly wound was healed. He performs great signs, so that he even makes fire come down from heaven on the earth in the sight of men. And he deceives those who dwell on the earth by those signs which he was granted to do in the sight of the beast, telling those who dwell on the earth to make an image to the beast who was wounded by the sword and lived. He was granted power to give breath to the image of the beast, that the image of the beast should both speak and cause as many as would not worship the image of the beast to be killed. He causes all, both small and great, rich and poor, free and slave, to receive a mark on their right hand or on their foreheads, and that no one may buy or sell except one who has the mark or the name of the beast, or the number of his name. Here is wisdom. Let him who has understanding calculate the number of the beast, for it is the number of a man: His number is 666.*

He will be the one who uproots three of the ten horns in the latter days.

| 1. | The false prophet arises after the ten horns come into power. This is a future event. | Daniel 7:24 |
|---|---|---|
| 2. | He will blaspheme God and will attempt to change the laws. This is a future event. | Daniel 7:25 |
| 3. | His ancestry is from the Selucid Kings, who came from one of the four generals of Alexander the Great. He is empowered by Satan and will perform the abomination of desolation against God and the Jewish people for the second time. *See discussion in this book in Chapter 5: Israel in the section Israel under Syrian and Roman Rule.* This is an historical event, however, we will see this horn reappear in the future. | Daniel 8:9-11 |

| 4. | I believe the visions of the evening and morning refer to history and future respectively. | Daniel 8:25-26 |
|----|---|---|
|    | When he rises against the Prince of princes and is broken without human means, | Daniel 2:45 |
|    | this will occur at the battle at Armageddon when he will meet Christ (Prince of princes), *the stone cut without hand* that will smite his kingdoms. | Daniel 12 |
|    | This whole scene is showing Antiochus Epiphanes who was the little horn that caused the desolation of abomination for Israel near 175 B.C., who will come again in the end times to repeat this horrible condition near the 1290 days spoken of in Daniel 12. This will be in the end times. Christ also spoke of this in Matthew 24:15. | |
| 5. | *The beast that you saw* refers to Antiochus Epiphanes in 175 B.C. therefore, the term used is past tense *was*; the term *is not* refers to the time when Antiochus Epiphanes is in the bottomless pit, during John's time and into our time; and *yet is* refers to when Antiochus Epiphanes comes back from the bottomless pit in the future. Of course the unbelievers who are dwelling on the earth would marvel when they see this event. In Revelation 17:9-13, we read that the beast that was, is not, is of the seven heads but will be the eighth head. This ties into Antiochus Epiphanes who was of the seven but when he comes again, he will be the eighth. | Revelation 17:8 |

## False Prophet's Kingdom

The false prophet continues to rule the same kingdom that was established by the antichrist. The first part of the kingdom consisted of seven heads representing the nations who enter a covenant, these being called the great harlot. The great harlot in turn is described as riding on the beast which is the antichrist's kingdom. The antichrist himself, will be empowered by Satan as will his entire kingdom of multiple nations (heads). In the latter part of his kingdom *he shall cause them to rule over many, and shall divide the land for gain.* (Daniel 11:39) This is when he grants authority to the ten kings over the land he has conquered during the war after the opening of the first seal. The ten kings are established close to mid-tribulation, when the false prophet takes over the rule of the kingdom. At this time he up-roots three of the ten horns which should leave eight, including himself. The false prophet's kingdom will be destroyed at Armageddon.

# Revelation Chapter 18

This is God's judgment on the atrocities that were committed during the existence of historical kingdoms. He calls the whole thing Babylon and also the mighty city. He is looking at all of the sins and summarizes how He sees her wickedness. He also says that the judgment of the world's system will come in one day; wherein He will burn her with fire.

The judgment of the harlot (Babylon the Great) will take place immediately prior to the battle at Armageddon. This world-wide system of abomination to God began during the time of the Babylonian empire and will continue to the end of the tribulation period, at which time the same historical nations will be united under covenant and will become the seven heads of the antichrist's kingdom. God refers to them as the harlot, and the entire life span of the system from its beginning, as the great city.

### Revelation 18:19
*"They threw dust on their heads and cried out, weeping and wailing, and saying, 'Alas, alas, that great city, in which all who had ships on the sea became rich by her wealth! For in one hour she is made desolate.'*

### Revelation 17:18
*And the woman whom you saw is that great city which reigns over the kings of the earth."*

The great city, which represents man's systems and lifestyles, will be destroyed by God in this judgment of the harlot.

### Revelation 18:21
*Then a mighty angel took up a stone like a great millstone and threw it into the sea, saying, "Thus with violence the*

*great city Babylon shall be thrown down, and shall not be found anymore.*

God will be praised in heaven for executing His judgment on the harlot.

### Revelation 19:2
*For true and righteous are His judgments, because He has judged the great harlot who corrupted the earth with her fornication; and He has avenged on her the blood of His servants shed by her.*

# Revelation Chapter 19

Here John has a vision of a major event that will take place in heaven, called the marriage of the Lamb. Christ will be the groom and the Church will be the bride. He also has a vision of the battle at Armageddon where both the antichrist and the false prophet are captured and cast into the lake of fire.

The marriage of the Lamb will take place in heaven following the judgment of the great harlot.

### Revelation 19:7
*Let us be glad and rejoice and give Him glory, for the marriage of the Lamb has come, and His wife has made herself ready.*

### Revelation 19:9
*Then he said to me, "Write: 'Blessed are those who are called to the marriage supper of the Lamb!'" And he said to me, "These are the true sayings of God.*

Compare the words with those found in Daniel.

### Daniel 12:12
*Blessed is he who waits, and comes to the one thousand three hundred and thirty-five days.*

These words show the judgment of the great harlot will occur near the end of the 75-day period, at the close of the tribulation period. We know this because it precedes the marriage of the Lamb, which will take place at this time, and it is followed by the battle at Armageddon.

## Revelation 19:11- Revelation 20:10

*Now I saw heaven opened, and behold, a white horse. And He who sat on him was called Faithful and True, and in righteousness He judges and makes war. His eyes were like a flame of fire, and on His head were many crowns. He had a name written that no one knew except Himself. He was clothed with a robe dipped in blood, and His name is called The Word of God. And the armies in heaven, clothed in fine linen, white and clean, followed Him on white horses. Now out of His mouth goes a sharp sword, that with it He should strike the nations. And He Himself will rule them with a rod of iron. He Himself treads the winepress of the fierceness and wrath of Almighty God. And He has on His robe and on His thigh a name written: KING OF KINGS AND LORD OF LORDS. Then I saw an angel standing in the sun; and he cried with a loud voice, saying to all the birds that fly in the midst of heaven, "Come and gather together for the supper of the great God, that you may eat the flesh of kings, the flesh of captains, the flesh of mighty men, the flesh of horses and of those who sit on them, and the flesh of all people, free and slave, both small and great." And I saw the beast, the kings of the earth, and their armies, gathered together to make war against Him who sat on the horse and against His army. Then the beast was captured, and with him the false prophet who worked signs in his presence, by which he deceived those who received the mark of the beast and those who worshiped his image. These two were cast alive into the lake of fire burning with brimstone. And the rest were killed with the sword which proceeded from the mouth of Him who sat on the horse. And all the birds were filled with their flesh.*

*Then I saw an angel coming down from heaven, having the key to the bottomless pit and a great chain in his hand. He laid hold of the dragon, that serpent of old, who is the Devil and Satan, and bound him for a thousand years; and he cast him into the bottomless pit, and shut him up, and set a seal on him, so that he should deceive the nations no more till the thousand years were finished. But after these things he must be released for a little while. And I saw thrones, and they sat on them, and judgment was committed to them. Then I saw the souls of those who had been beheaded for their witness to Jesus and for the word of God, who had not worshiped the beast or his image, and had not received his mark on their foreheads or on their hands. And they lived and reigned with Christ for a thousand years. But the rest of the dead did not live again until the thousand years were finished. This is the first resurrection. Blessed and holy is he who has part in the first resurrection. Over such the second death has no power, but they shall be priests of God and of Christ, and shall reign with Him a thousand years. Now when the thousand years have expired, Satan will be released from his prison and will go out to deceive the nations which are in the four corners of the earth, Gog and Magog, to gather them together to battle, whose number is as the sand of the sea. They went up on the breadth of the earth and surrounded the camp of the saints and the beloved city. And fire came down from God out of heaven and devoured them. The devil, who deceived them, was cast into the lake of fire and brimstone where the beast and the false prophet are. And they will be tormented day and night forever and ever.*

# Revelation Chapter 20

The first event in this chapter is the binding of Satan in chains and the casting of him into the bottomless pit, where he remains throughout the millennium. At this time, Christ will conduct the *judgment* of nations. The souls who were beheaded for their witness to Jesus and the Word of God, and who did not receive the mark of the beast will be allowed to go into the millennium.

There are many references in the Word concerning the millennium, which is the last kingdom on the earth; it will last for a period of 1000 years and there will be peace on the earth.

### Revelation 11:15

*Then the seventh angel sounded: And there were loud voices in heaven, saying, "The kingdoms of this world have become the kingdoms of our Lord and of His Christ, and He shall reign forever and ever!*

### Revelation 20:4

*And I saw thrones, and they sat on them, and judgment was committed to them. Then I saw the souls of those who had been beheaded for their witness to Jesus and for the word of God, who had not worshiped the beast or his image, and had not received his mark on their foreheads or on their hands. And they lived and reigned with Christ for a thousand years.*

The 1000 years of peace will take place after Satan is bound in chains and placed in the bottomless pit. After the battle at Armageddon, Christ will stay on Mount Zion and the 144,000 Jews that were sealed in their foreheads by God at mid-tribulation will be with Him ready to enter the millennium, which is the start of the everlasting kingdom of God. It is the kingdom and the land that was promised to Abraham and Jacob.

# Revelation Chapter 21

God will be creating a new heaven and a new earth, for the first heaven and the first earth passed away and there was no more sea.

### Revelation 21:2-4
*Then I, John, saw the holy city, New Jerusalem, coming down out of heaven from God, prepared as a bride adorned for her husband. And I heard a loud voice from heaven saying, "Behold, the tabernacle of God is with men, and He will dwell with them, and they shall be His people. God Himself will be with them and be their God. And God will wipe away every tear from their eyes; there shall be no more death, nor sorrow, nor crying. There shall be no more pain, for the former things have passed away."*

New Jerusalem is a new city, as God said *I will make all things new*, the first new thing mentioned. This new city is called the Lamb's wife and only those found written in the Book of Life can go in and out of the city. The first bride of Christ was the church, all who believed in Him. New Jerusalem will descend from heaven to the new earth. One can, therefore, conclude the new earth is part of the new heaven; in this way believers of the bride of Christ in heaven can access the city on the new earth.

# Revelation Chapter 22

The river of life being the water of life, proceeds from the throne of God and of the Lamb and on either side of the river there will be the tree of life. I believe that the Throne of God will be in the new heaven, because the Throne of God today exists in the highest layer of the heavens. This scene, therefore, relates to the new heaven. The glory of God will provide light in heaven where we will reign with bliss with God forever. The book of Revelation closes with John's and Christ's words of encouragement to all believers to keep the words of the prophecy given in the book of Revelation.

# Closing Remarks

In the books of Ezekiel, Daniel, and Revelation we have studied historical world events and world events that are to come in the future. To rightly divide the Word of Truth one must know the chronological order of the events and also the meaning of the words that describe them. The chronological order of the major events are shown on a simplified chart included as part of this book. As much as possible the author has employed a literal interpretation except for God's special names and phrases that He gave to help us understand the context. In those parts which are more difficult to understand, God often used the word *mystery*. The cross-referencing of scriptures is an aid to keep the meaning in its proper context. I sincerely trust the reader will receive a clear understanding of the prophecies given in these books. May your faith be increased when you see the accuracy and truth in the Word of God, and may you have a comfort through the peace that passes understanding that only God can give. Surely all of us have a hope that we can enter into God's rest and obtain everlasting life.

LaVergne, TN USA
13 August 2010
193260LV00001B/36/P